"

A Powerhouse for Sustainable Growth. So much so, I had to have Mel on my Forbes Books podcast to reveal her secrets.

David Radlo, Forbes Books, US

"

A captivating, page-turning book. I learned more from this book than completing an entire sustainability business strategy course at Harvard Business School. That course at Harvard was excellent. This book is better. Everybody should read this.

Matt Deasy, B Corp Leader and Business Sustainability Consultant, Portugal

"

An outstanding achievement. A genuinely transformational impact approach. It has changed how I think about the subject forever.

Mark Logan, Chief Entrepreneurship Officer Scottish Government, Professor, Former COO Skyscanner, UK

"

A must-read for anyone seeking inspiration and motivation to address global issues head-on. A truly exceptional book.

Igor Filart, Senior Manager ASICS Technology, Australia

"

Dr van de Velde's doctoral thesis is outstanding and a worthy winner of the Adam Smith Prize for PhD Excellence.
Dr Haugh, Research Director at the Centre for Social Innovation, Cambridge University, UK

"

Finally, a tool to help identify effective impact initiatives. Making positive impact and delivering profits may seem paradoxical, but it is possible. Melanie has solved this with her simple, easy-to-adopt model to help businesses to create powerful impact strategies.
Mark Fallows, Founder, Fabrica Collective & The Impossible Network, US

"

Melanie van de Velde's book LEAD LIKE A GENIUS inspired me with her evidence-based work on balancing people, planet, and profit. I love the key insight to balance impact with the GOOD profit drivers!
Robert van der Laan, Lecturer Rotterdam University of Applied Sciences, former PwC Corporate Responsibility Leader EMEA, The Netherlands

"

Amazing insights, this is the need of the hour.
Inir Pinheiro, Founder Grassroutes, India

"

Justice without freedom is captivity.

Freedom without justice is destruction.

But with freedom and justice, humanity can thrive.

Melanie van de Velde

To Conor, Bean, and Amie,

For I hope you, your children, and all children,
will live your lives in a thriving and harmonious world.

About the author

The nine-year-old Melanie van de Velde was asked what problem she would like to solve when she grew up. She answered that she wanted to help people who were living in poverty. At the time, she had yet to see severe deprivation first-hand, but in the years since, she's travelled extensively and the suffering she's witnessed has only strengthened her ambition in childhood.

Dr Van de Velde was awarded the Adam Smith Prize for PhD Excellence. Nominated for the prize by the Research Director at the Centre for Social Innovation at Cambridge University, her thesis was the source of many insights in this book.

Her other academic achievements include an MBA with Distinction from the University of Glasgow in the UK, and an MSc in Industrial Engineering at the University of Twente in The Netherlands.

With a diverse CV, Dr Van de Velde has managed Asia Pacific markets at a multi-billion-dollar tech company. She's worked in senior management at IT start-ups. And she's run a fashion business to empower young women without an education in a Nairobi slum.

With Big Tree Global Ltd, she helps business leaders with the tools and insights to create effective impact strategies that lead to business growth and genuinely transform our world for the better. B Journeys Ltd, her other startup, aims to create economic opportunities in some of the most deprived, remote, and, simultaneously, stunning parts of our world.

Raised in a small town in the Netherlands, she now lives with her partner and children in Scotland's largest city.

Thank you

Reading this book, a final time, I feel hugely grateful to have met amazing humans on my journey. People who, amidst the often-tragic events in the news, spend their days making a real difference to our world. I am in awe of what they do and how well they do it. They fill me with hope that we will evolve to a much better world, if solutions like theirs become more part of the mainstream. Thank you for sharing your valuable insights, lessons learned, and for leading the way.

The many hours spent on my research and writing this book have been a privilege, hugely inspiring, a real joy, and - at times - a hard slog. As it feels like crossing the finish line of a marathon typing the last words in the book, I feel immensely thankful for everyone's support helping me get there.

A massive thanks to Professor Yunus, Willemijn Verloop, Peter Holbrook, Liam Black, Henk Jan Beltman, Sandra Ballij, Robert van der Laan, Jeroen Govaard, Sharon Veerbeek, Mark Parsons, Thom Kenrick, Inir Pinheiro, Uday Nanda, Duttatraya Kondarv, Maavshi Sarabai, Simon Boyle, Sonya Blackwood, David Stirling, Michael Chance, Jan Seymour, Leon Seraphin, Gerry Higgins, Ruud Zandvliet, Hans Cornelissen, Hans Vugts, Margaret McGovern, Sir Tom Hunter, Josh Littlejohn, Ronald Ron Coyle, Lorraine McLaren, Maurice McCafferty, Lynsey McLean, Graham Bell, Lesley Fuller, Camillo Doornekamp, Mike Britton, Steve Morgan, Josh Hawkins, George Roberts, Eduardo Balarezo, Georgina Marten, Gaby Aguina, Mark Logan, William Richardson, and Brieuc Saffré for sharing your valuable wisdom and experiences that underpin many of the insights in this book.

Thank you, Professor Mason, Professor Gordon, and Professor D'Angelo for guiding me throughout my research and encouraging me to dig deeper even still. It was just the right push to discover the crucial insights. Professor Morgan-Thomas, for being enthusiastic throughout. And Dr Haugh, for your rigorous review and valuable feedback.

To Simon and Katie, for hugely generously offering to host a launch event at your amazing Brigade Bar & Bistro in London. Your support means a lot. To Sandra, for your unwavering whirlwind of enthusiasm that makes me smile when I think about it. To Inir, Uday, and Eduardo, for not only sharing valuable insights but also being exceptionally kind and generous hosts.

A big thanks to Ben, Lucy, Caitlin, Sabrina, Riemke, Becky, David, Clare, Jo, Anna, Sudheen, Alisha, Pranav, Jennifer, James, Sarah, Brian, and Rob for your amazing support to the book launch. To David, for going above and beyond proofreading the manuscript.

To Thom, Robert, Matt, Dr Haugh, Sarah, Bruno, Mark, Inir, Gert, Jules, Jamie, Rebecca, Avi, Kirsteen, Jurjen, Dani, Valda, Sue, Jennie, Anna, Hester, Kerry, Edwin, Michael, and Conor, for being there and your awesome support and endorsements. And Jude, for all your help – you're the best!

To Janet, for your interest and support – it means more than you know.

To all my friends and family, for being lovely humans, I feel very lucky to have you in my life. To my mum and my dad, who sadly passed away unexpectedly a few months ago, for everything.

And last but not least, a huge thank you to David, for all your support in many ways, you have been amazing. To Conor, thank you for being sweet and for ploughing through it. To lovely Bean, for cheering me on and your talented creative eyes. And a huge, big cuddle to Amie for your beautiful drawing that you were adamant about making it into the book (and to make sure to mention that you are my daughter). I'm very glad it has.

Contents

LEAD LIKE A GENIUS

How to outgrow the competition
and transform our world

Melanie van de Velde, PhD, MBA, MSc

A truckload of shoes

One early Saturday morning about 15 years ago, my friend Jennie and I were about to join a 10K run in Kibera, one of the world's largest slums, home to more than a million people in Nairobi. While hanging about at the starting area, news spread fast that a truck was arriving nearby, loaded with fancy trainers to be handed out as a donation by a major sports brand.

Up until that moment, it had been a calm, sunny Saturday morning. A happy vibe hung in the air in anticipation of the race. But with the news of the truck the mood darkened. Larger crowds gathered, and people started taking on strategic positions on walls. We could see some people grabbing hold of rocks. I could only imagine that they did so in case fights would break out. Jennie and I decided to leave and go for a run elsewhere.

I don't know how the truck's arrival unfolded. I imagine the lucky ones who ended up with a pair of shoes would have likely sold them. First, out of safety. Walking about with expensive trainers is not the best idea in Kibera, which harbours some of the warmest-hearted and most generous people you will ever meet, but also some people who are – quite understandably – desperate. The average life expectancy in Kibera is 30 years old.[1] It is essentially a city of children and young people, with not many parents around to look after them. And second, the money to be gained from selling the shoes was probably needed more urgently for other things, like food, a school uniform, or antibiotics for a child sick with pneumonia.

Sending a truckload of trainers, whether driven by a PR campaign or from the heart, was a kind gesture. However, it shows the need for a better understanding of the issues and how to solve them effectively.

---

[1] *The Guardian*, 2019

What took me to Nairobi was a strong feeling that I could not stand by watching people in our world living in poverty. As much as I loved working in a brilliant technology company based in the South of France, that feeling became stronger on my frequent visits to India, one of the markets I looked after. It didn't feel right to be ferried between a hotel and offices, passing the many children and people living in slums and on the streets. How could I put my energy into talking about new software launches while these families were facing such horrendous and life-threatening conditions?

It was not clear to me if and how I could make any genuine difference. But I did know for sure that I did not want to look back one day as an old lady not having tried.

The path this has taken me down, so far, has taught me a lot. It has taught me the beauty of working with children and young women in the Kibera slum towards a better future. It also taught me how challenging it can be to try to build a solid commercial platform at the same time.

Years of looking deeper into how we can best address our global issues, like poverty, have opened my eyes more to the other key injustices in our world, like rising inequality, social exclusion, climate change, and pollution. I have learned how these issues are linked and that they are much more connected to how we do business than I had ever suspected.

Increasingly, it has become clear that business leaders can offer a significant part of the solution to our global challenges; and, if they don't, that most of our global issues are unlikely to be resolved, and we can expect many to worsen and others to arise.

It has been a tremendous honour to learn from business leaders worldwide who work with their heart and soul to make a positive impact across the range of global issues that we face. I have loved seeing the sparkle in their eyes talking about their journeys, taking the many challenges they face on the chin.

As Sandra Ballij, founder of Ctalents, who features as one of the genius leaders in this book, says: "I don't know anyone who regrets going down the path of making an impact."

Witnessing how the lives of people, who have been dealt unfortunate cards, can be transformed has sent shivers down my spine.

Last – and perhaps most importantly – my own experiences working in and with companies and years of research into impact initiatives from around the world have taught me that 'doing something' is often not the best answer. It matters what you do and how you do it. Some initiatives have significantly better outcomes than others. And some end up doing more harm than good, despite the best of intentions.

So, a key question is *why* are certain initiatives far more successful than others in tackling the biggest issues we face as humanity, even though they have a similar mission and context? Why do some have a 200-400% better impact return on investment and gain more significant competitive advantages compared to most? What do they do differently?

As it turns out, those with the best outcomes have the exact same patterns in common, regardless of their size or sector. This book provides a simple guide to apply the key ingredients for better outcomes in your context. It outlines the insights and tools needed to gain a competitive edge in terms of better business growth, productivity, brand value, and resilience; and, at the same time, better results in terms of genuinely transforming our world.

Children living on the street in Mumbai, India.

Impact is vital for business

Ninety nine percent of CEOs say they believe sustainability is essential to the future success of their business.[2] Customers, employees, and investors, particularly the younger, increasingly favour companies that have a positive impact on our world.[3] As the younger generations are becoming a larger part of a company's eco system, the value it provides to society is expected to become only more important.

With sustainability shifting to a more mature stage, it is getting clear however that not all strategies lead to the intended impact, nor competitive advantages. Whether the benefits that can be gained materialise depends on authenticity and trust. It depends on how effectively you make a difference. And it depends on at what stage a business comes on board in pursuing not only profits, but also a positive impact on our world.

Studies show that companies that get impact right have begun to outgrow their competitors. A Deloitte study shows that purpose driven companies grow three times faster than their peers.[4] The superior growth rates can for a large part be explained by better customer retention and referral rates. Tony's Chocolonely has taken the chocolate sector by storm, benefiting from a high customer referral rate, partly because of its mission to eradicate child labour on cocoa plantations in West Africa.[5] Costco demonstrates how positive impact can contribute to exceptional customer retention rates, and in turn sales and profit rates, revenue growth, and stock gains that are far superior to its rivals as we will see in Chapter Four.[6]

---

[2] PwC, 2019; UN Global Compact, 2019
[3] BlackRock, 2019; Morgan Stanley, 2018; Reichheld et al., 2023; Sisodia, Wolfe, and Sheth, 2014; Whelan & Kronthal-Sacco, 2019; Workplace Culture Trends, 2018
[4] Deloitte, 2019; Whelan & Kronthal-Sacco, 2019
[5] Tony's Chocolonely Annual Report, 2022
[6] Costco Annual Report, 2022

"

If you're not a sustainable company in the next decade, you will be out. Or at least behind and losing ground in almost every industry.

Bracken Darrel, former CEO of Logitech [7]

[7] Interview Bracken Darrell by Mark Fallows, The Impossible Network Podcast,
https://theimpossiblenetwork.com/podcast/bracken-darrell/

PwC reports that 90% of our global citizens expect businesses to contribute to the United Nations Sustainable Development Goals (SDGs).[8] The UN has agreed to these SDGs as our world's key priorities, including climate change, pollution, poverty, and rising inequality. Increasingly, customers say they want to buy from companies with a positive impact on our world, currently estimated at around 80% to 90%.[9]

Aside from better growth rates, organisations that get their impact right, experience other significant business benefits. They are more productive, with more engaged teams, and tend to be better at attracting talented staff. Eighty six percent of millennials indicate they would even take a pay cut to work for an employer with strong values.[10]

And finally, companies that are strong at sustainability tend to experience an increase in their brand value. Kantar reports that purpose-driven brands have experienced a valuation of plus 175%.[11] GE reported a $6 billion USD increase in brand value three years after launching its Eco Imagination range.[12] According to a Bank of America Merrill Lynch's report, ESG companies, with above-average environmental and social profiles, have a higher return on equity, are more resilient, and are significantly less likely to declare bankruptcy.[13]

> Would you like your business to take a leadership position in tackling certain global issues as an 'innovator' or 'early adopter', be part of an 'early or late majority', or wait until (upcoming) regulations require compliance?
>
> What will more likely lead to competitive advantages or disadvantages?

---

[8] PwC, 2015a
[9] Eon, 2020; Forbes, 2018; PwC, 2015a
[10] Workplace Culture Trends, 2018
[11] Kantar, 2020
[12] Porter and Kramer, 2011
[13] BofAML, 2019

99%

of CEOs believe
sustainability is important
to their future success.

Purpose driven brands
have experienced a
valuation of

+ 175%

Purpose-driven
companies grow

three times

faster.

Sources: UN Global Compact, 2019; PwC, 2019; KPMG, 2020; Deloitte, 2019; Kantar, 2020.

One of the most encouraging examples to me is the story of Unilever. Compared to other impact leaders that are featured in this book, it is not as far ahead on the sustainability curve. However, its sustainability efforts have been significantly more progressive than most multinationals over the past 12 years. And the commercial benefits speak for themselves.

After years of low or no growth, Unilever started its 'Sustainable Living Plan' in 2010. Seven years later its revenue was up by 33%, with its stock outperforming its peers.[14] Unilever's sustainable living brands drove 70% of its overall turnover growth at that stage.[15]

At that point, its rival Kraft Heinz, owned by 3G and Berkshire Hathaway, offered a lucrative takeover bid of 18% over the market price. The bid sent a message to investors that there was money to be made by cutting the costs involved with Unilever's sustainability efforts.

3G is well known for slashing costs to increase short-term profits. In a 2017 article, the *Financial Times* called this "a model that ultimately destroys business by starving them of investment". Companies bought by 3G, such as SAB Miller with water and human rights projects in Africa, were squeezed by cost cuttings following their takeover. There was much public support for Unilever not to sell to Kraft Heinz, and ultimately, it declined.

Over the 10 years that followed every dollar invested in Unilever has led to a 400% higher return than Kraft Heinz.[16] Paul Polman, Unilever's CEO at the time, explains that the company's sustainability strategy gave it more resilience, contributing to its superior return. An example is its ability to reinvent supply chains faster to make hand sanitisers during the Covid pandemic in 2020, having built more trust with its partners over the years. Meanwhile, Kraft Heinz struggled during this period, having to write off $15 billion USD.

---

[14] Polman & Winston, 2021
[15] Unilever, 2018
[16] Polman & Winston, 2021; Unilever, 2018

It doesn't always work out well

Not all sustainability strategies create lasting positive impact. Some initiatives achieve a far better impact return across the sustainability landscape than most. And some create more significant competitive advantages than others.

The Unilever versus Kraft Heinz story highlights a choice between short-term gains or opting for a business that flourishes long term. There are other critical choices to be made however in leading a business to success in terms of commercial outcomes as well as the impact on our world.

How can you balance profit maximisation with creating value for society? When should you prioritise purpose over profits and vice versa? And on what grounds? If you have a grant, several grants or a million to invest with your company, how can you best make a difference? Why are some initiatives far more successful in tackling our key global issues compared to others with a similar mission and context?

I have spent many years trying to understand the answers to these questions better, working in and with companies, and running a business in the Kibera slum in Nairobi, that provided training and employment opportunities to young women without an education. An experience that I loved but that was very challenging at the same time. It made me want to learn more about different types of initiatives from around the globe and understand what works well versus less well. This became the driving force for my PhD research, which was awarded the Adam Smith Prize for PhD Excellence, nominated by the Research Director at the Centre for Social Innovation at Cambridge University.

The research included a comparison of some of the world's leading examples and an in-depth study of what sets their superior outcomes apart from others with a similar context. Further insights were gained through interviewing many prominent experts with a wealth of experience, such as Professor Yunus, Nobel Peace Prize Laureate and Founder of the

Grameen Bank. A hugely inspirational example of a profitable bank in Bangladesh that has lifted more than 9 million mothers and their families out of poverty through its micro-credits.

What I discovered is that those with the best outcomes have the exact same underlying patterns, regardless of their size or sector. The secrets to the best outcomes at its deepest level can be distilled into four words: 'LEAD LIKE A GENIUS', as will be unravelled throughout the chapters.

Most sustainability frameworks are detailed, and/ or compliance focused. This can serve a good purpose, such as validation and certification. However, such detailed tools tend to make it hard to see the most innovative and effective solutions; or to identify the 20% of initiatives that make 80% of the difference and lead to the best competitive advantages.

In this book you will find a step-by-step guide on using the key ingredients to generate impact for the best outcomes. I refer mainly to a business context, but many of the insights also apply to other types of organisations. While the framework is straightforward to use, it underpins the world's most successful impact strategies. If each organisation applies the framework, it can not only guide business leaders in creating a better return, but it would profoundly change the course of history. It could fix much of poverty, inequality, social exclusion, climate change, and pollution at its root; and prevent many other future global issues that are on their way.

I hope that this book will inspire you to take a step back and reflect on how you can create impact for the best outcomes. The best outcomes for your business. And the best outcomes that truly transform our world.

Chapter One

Creating the best outcomes

Illustration by Silvan Borer.

What makes a 'genius leader'?

What makes a genius? Your initial thought – like mine – may be 'an exceptional IQ'. Interestingly, what sets some of the best-known geniuses in our history apart from others is that they think differently, with one common trait in particular: their brains look at problems in a unique way, compared to what is considered natural to the human brain.

When our brains are confronted with opposites, they are wired to focus on either one or the other, but not both simultaneously. Back in 1979 psychiatrist Albert Rothenberg discovered that this is precisely what geniuses do differently.[17]

Rothenberg's study at Harvard University revealed that what people like Einstein, Picasso, van Gogh, Edison, Da Vinci, and Mozart had in common was 'the pursuit of a unity of opposites'. For example, Einstein played with the simultaneity of objects in motion and at rest; Mozart engaged concordance and discordance in music; and Picasso sought visual images that conveyed light and dark. Rothenberg named the use of opposites 'Janusian thinking' after Janus, a Roman God with two faces, each looking in the opposite direction.

Business and management scientists suggest increasingly that the solution to several complex problems can be found in the combination of opposites, as opposed to an 'either/ or' perspective. According to these scientists, balancing opposites as part of a whole instead of separating them leads to far better outcomes by creating synergies and virtuous cycles. They refer to this as 'paradox theory'.[18]

---

[17] Rothenberg, 1979
[18] Poole & Van de Ven, 1989; Schad et al., 2016; Smith & Tracey, 2016

It felt like a real 'aha!' when I compared the critical patterns in my data with these theories. This is precisely what companies that create the best outcomes for both 'profits and purpose' have in common. What they do superbly well is that *they pursue both profits and purpose as part of a whole*. They do not concentrate predominantly on maximising profits and see their impact on society and planet as a separate aim to 'give back'. Nor do they pursue an environmental or social purpose and focus on profits secondary. While this might sound puzzling, this will become much clearer throughout the book with examples in a variety of contexts.

Let's start by looking more closely at 'purpose'. What does it mean for companies to create positive value for our planet and societies? How does business relate to the key global challenges that humanity is facing? And what type of impact strategies are more versus less effective in tackling these issues?

Truly fixing our global issues

Imagine you're running a nice warm bath and, while it's filling up, you take a phone call that turns out to take longer than expected. When you step back into the bathroom, the bath has begun to overflow. What do you do? Most people would turn off the tap (or pull the plug). No one would mop up the floor but leave the tap running. It simply would not make any sense.

Yet, when it comes to the mountains of plastic entering our oceans each year, or climate change, and our other global issues, too many initiatives deal merely with the symptoms of these issues. They are investing metaphorically in 'mopping up' without closing the tap at the same time.

Genuinely fixing our key global issues requires several parties to play a fitting role. Such as policies and legislation by governments and global institutions; education; and support by NGOs. Fixing our global issues long term however requires business leaders to play a critical part. As in the words of Antionio Guterres, Secretary-General of the UN: "Collaboration with business is crucial when it comes to fighting climate change and eradicating all extreme poverty by 2030, and we're not on track."[19]

Business leaders are particularly well placed to tackle the root causes across the biggest challenges we are facing in our world, instead of alleviating the symptoms. Let's use the 17 SDGs, our key global challenges as defined by the UN as a starting point. These include No poverty; Zero hunger; Good health and wellbeing; Quality education; Gender equality; Clean water and sanitation; Affordable and clean energy; Decent work and economic growth; Innovation; Reduced inequalities; Sustainable cities and communities; Responsible consumption and production; Climate action; Life below water; Life on land; Peace, justice and strong institutions; and Partnerships to achieve the goals.[20]

---

[19] https://sdgs.un.org/goals
[20] United Nations, 2019

In the words of former UN Secretary-General Ban Ki-moon, the SDGs are the "shared vision of humanity".[21]

If we look at each of the goals individually, it can be hard to see the bigger picture and identify how to best invest towards lasting, significant impact. Several business leaders have mentioned during my workshops how addressing the 17 SDGs and subgoals can seem quite overwhelming. Once we see how the goals relate to each other, we can identify the core opportunity areas where a business can tackle the root causes of the goals structurally and effectively. Addressing certain SDGs leads to a return of $20 to $40 USD for every $1 spent, compared to less than $10 return by spending money equally across all SDGs.[22]

As an example, let's look at the first six SDGs: 1) No poverty; 2) Zero hunger; 3) Good health and wellbeing; 4) Quality education; 5) Gender equality; and 6) Clean water and sanitation. We could spread our investment across each of these six goals separately. For instance, we could improve gender equality within our organisation, and donate to charities related to poverty, hunger, medical care, schools, and sanitation.

To address poverty-related issues, many companies adopt the 'buy-one-give-one-model', or similarly the 'buy-one-give-a-percentage-model'. Like Warby Parker distributing a pair of glasses to someone in need for every pair purchased. Or TOMS Shoes, which was one of the first to adopt this model by donating a pair of shoes to a child for each pair a consumer buys.

Giving glasses, shoes, or other donations can provide crucial temporary relief. But as Bethlehem Tilahun Alemu, the Founder of SoleRebels, an international footwear company based in Ethiopia, asks: "If you give a child a pair of shoes and it grows out of it, then what does it have? But if you give parents a job, the whole family will always have shoes."[23]

---

[21] United Nations, 2015b
[22] Lomborg, 2015
[23] Timmerman, 2023

SoleRebels, Africa's fastest-growing footwear brand, takes a more structural approach in addressing poverty. It has opened production facilities in areas that need economic development, paying employees three times the industry average wage. It enables parents to buy their children not just shoes but also food, school uniforms, glasses, or medical care. This strategy does not only tackle the first UN SDG, 'No poverty', but it has positive knock-on effects on related SDGs such as 'Zero Hunger' and 'Health and Wellbeing'.

Moreover, by providing economic opportunities in these areas, local communities are in a better position to invest in schools and clean water facilities and sanitation. This in turn can help to improve gender equality, with women and girls being responsible for water collection in 70% of families that lack sanitation.[24]

Charitable donations can be essential in some situations like emergencies. They can further provide vital temporary relief, as I witnessed myself with our programmes to support children in the Kibera slum with food packages, school uniforms, and school fees. But unless we start addressing the root cause of poverty at the same time, it is like mopping up whilst leaving the tap running.

In addition, donations can cause more harm than good in some contexts. When second-hand clothing donations ramped up in Africa, more than 50% of people in the local textile industries lost their jobs as a consequence.[25] When charitable donations are used long-term, these can also be found to cause adverse psychological impacts, including shame, inferiority, powerlessness, humiliation, fear, hopelessness, depression, social isolation and voicelessness.[26]

---

[24] UNESCO, 2022; WHO, 2023
[25] Frazer, 2008
[26] Corbett and Fikkert, 2009

Bethlehem Tilahun Alemu, Founder of SoleRebels, adds: "Aid and charity in almost all their formats and configurations won't ever create jobs; cannot and never will create sustained prosperity."[27]

The same concept applies to climate change or other global issues. When we focus our efforts on symptoms, we can keep investing money, time, and energy in dealing with the problem. But when we fix the root cause, we turn off the tap and no longer need to keep mopping up.

In the context of the plastic marine crisis, we can support initiatives working tirelessly to scoop up plastic from our oceans. But with more than 525,600 truckloads full of plastic entering our seas each year at an increasing rate, ocean clean-up initiatives are a losing game.[28] The situation can only improve discernably, when we start tackling plastic waste at its root.

There are essentially four key areas where companies can close the tap of humanity's biggest challenges, the UN SDGs. I have summarised these four opportunity areas in what I call the 'IMPACT Wheel'. Over the course of the next four chapters, we will look at each of the four quadrants of the IMPACT Wheel: Q1 Empowerment (a wider scope than 'being inclusive'); Q2 Just Payments (different from 'fairtrade' as will become evident in Chapter Three); Q3 Planet; and Q4 Health and wellbeing.

We will look at compelling examples from around the world in each of the quadrants of the IMPACT Wheel; and we will understand why they achieve better outcomes than others – both in terms of profits and impactful results. You will discover questions that can be asked to tease out impact initiatives as part of your business, as part of your supply chain, and as part of a wider context. Like the waves that are generated by dropping a pebble in the water, the circles of the IMPACT Wheel symbolise the ripples that these types of initiatives can create across our world by not only tackling the root cause of the issues, but also by creating synergies and knock-on effects.

---

[27] Wharton, 2023
[28] Ellen McArthur Foundation, 2022; Jambeck et al. 2013

Q1. Empowerment   **Q2. Just Payments**

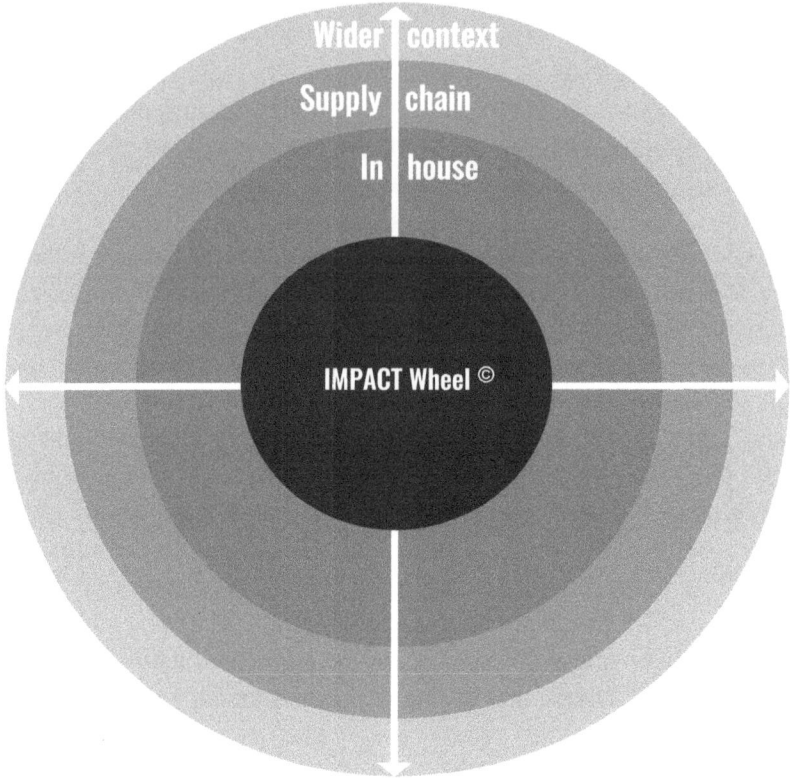

Wider context

Supply chain

In house

IMPACT Wheel ©

Q3. Planet   **Q4. Health & wellbeing**

The IMPACT Wheel

In a nutshell

1. Impact initiatives with better outcomes than most 'lead like a genius' by pursuing profits and purpose as part of a whole. They do not focus predominantly on maximising profits with a separate environmental or social mission, nor do they forget to incorporate important commercial drivers towards profits.

2. Impact initiatives are more effective if they tackle the root cause of our key global and local issues instead of addressing the symptoms.

3. There are four key impact opportunity areas where companies can tackle the root causes of the UN SDGs as part of their business model. These areas make up the four quadrants of the IMPACT Wheel. We will look at global best practices in each quadrant across the next four chapters and questions to identify similar practices in your context.

4. Developing impact initiatives in the four areas of the IMPACT Wheel enables companies to tackle global issues structurally at their root *and* create synergies and positive knock-on effects on related issues.

Let's start with the first quadrant 'Empowerment'.

Chapter Two

Empowerment

Q1. Empowerment

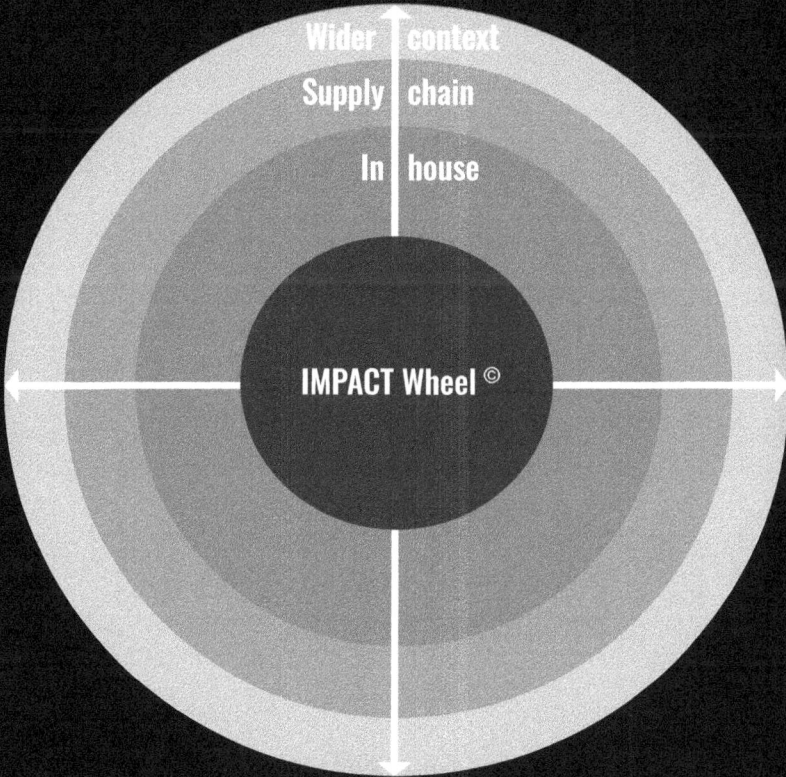

Wider context
Supply chain
In house

IMPACT Wheel ©

The United Nations has defined eradicating poverty as the number one priority for humanity and has issued an objective to eradicate extreme poverty everywhere by 2030. While improvements have been made, we are far from achieving this goal. Here are five harrowing statistics as to where we currently are:

1. An estimated 700 million people live in extreme poverty on less than $2.15 USD per day. The world's poorest people bear the steepest consequences of the rising food and energy prices and the Covid pandemic, with income losses twice as high as the world's richest.[29]

2. Half of our world's population lives below the poverty line of $6.85 USD per day, struggling to meet basic needs like health, education, and access to water and sanitation.[30]

3. Poverty affects children the most, with 20% of children under five living in extreme poverty globally.[31] More than five million children die before their fifth birthday each year. Most of these five million deaths are a result of poverty related issues such as a lack of good healthcare during pregnancy and childbirth, or the threat to infants of pneumonia, diarrhoea, malaria, poor nutrition, and hunger.[32]

4. As many as 160 million children are engaged in child labour globally, with 79 million exposed to its worst forms (modern slavery, trafficking, prostitution, and work that likely harms the health or safety of children).[33]

5. 244 million children are out of school. Women and girls are responsible for water collection in 70% of families that lack sanitation.[34]

---

[29] World Bank, 2022a
[30] World Bank, 2022b
[31] UN, 2023
[32] UN, 2023
[33] ILO, 2020
[34] UNESCO, 2022; WHO, 2023

2.5 million

5 million

Average global annual
total Covid-19 deaths.

(2020 & 2021)

Poverty related deaths
of children < 5 years old.

(Each year)

Sources: Oxford OurWorldInData, 2023; UN, 2023.

Relative poverty (when households receive 50% less than average household incomes) exists in most countries on our planet. In the UK, one of the world's wealthiest countries, more than 4 million children – a third of all children – live in relative poverty. This figure was expected to rise even before Covid-19.[35] Many of these children are reported to live in temporary accommodation, go to school hungry, have rickets (a disease related to vitamin deficiency), and have poor dental health.[36] Children in more impoverished families in the UK are 300% more likely to experience mental health issues at 11 years old than children growing up in families with average incomes.[37]

Poverty can seem insurmountable, but so did apartheid, or women not being allowed to vote, in the past. Solutions that genuinely tackle poverty and social exclusion already exist, but still need to be adopted sufficiently by the mainstream. While some initiatives are effective; others are less so. We tend to be drawn naturally to want to provide temporary relief through, for example, charitable donations. However, businesses and other organisations are well-positioned to tackle poverty and social exclusion more structurally.

There are excellent examples from around the world that fix the root cause of poverty by empowering people and communities in various ways.

If you lived in poverty with your family, would you rather be given glasses, shoes, or other donations for your children, or an opportunity to earn a living and be able to buy the things that your family needs?

---

[35] Social Metrics Commission, 2019
[36] McCall, 2016
[37] McCall, 2016

A hand up

Professor Muhammad Yunus beams of energy and charisma when we meet at an event in London. Hordes of reporters are trying to get a moment with the Nobel Peace Prize Laureate. When we finally get a quiet place for our interview the Founder of the Grameen Bank refers to people in poverty as "bonsai people". He explains: "I say poor people are bonsai people, there is nothing wrong with the seed. If you planted it in the right place, it would be as tall as anybody else. The society, the theory didn't give them the space."

Imagine that you are in an accident tomorrow and end up in a wheelchair or lose your eyesight. How would you feel if your skill set was cast aside suddenly, and you were left feeling marginalised from much of society? Imagine if, after years of sitting at home, someone came along and gave you the opportunity to use your talents again and regain your confidence, independence, and livelihood.

Or imagine that, after a series of unfortunate events, you lose your home with no one to fall back on. You end up sleeping rough, and your life spirals down. Imagine that one day, someone walks up to you, sees your potential, and gives you a safe, supportive place to retrain in something you love so you can rebuild your life.

There are entrepreneurs in this world who do precisely that. Each business leader can choose to make a difference to people's lives. For some, it is an overriding business mission that lights a fire in their heart and makes their eyes sparkle when they talk about what they do. It can equally be a small part of your business or organisation. If most organisations engaged in this way, we would tackle much of our world's poverty and social exclusion. Interestingly, as we will see later, doing it the right way also turns out to be beneficial from a business perspective.

Poverty is not only about having an insufficient income. It impacts social exclusion, self-esteem, and mental and physical health. Poverty deprives people of the freedom to contribute their unique potential.[38] Empowerment means the removal of unjust inequalities so individuals can make their own choices over improving their lives.[39]

Our training and employment opportunities for young women in the Kibera slum made me see more clearly how business leaders can offer people a far more effective solution out of poverty compared to giving 'handouts'. Donations can bring crucial temporary relief, and, in some contexts, it is the only solution. But, in many cases, this approach fails to fix anything long-term, nor does it create an upward spiral of confidence, self-esteem, security and a good quality of life.

The first part of the solution to addressing poverty and social exclusion structurally is giving people a 'hand up' by empowering them to use their potential. Empowerment is different from 'being inclusive'. While social inclusion can be a part of your empowerment strategy, the question 'how can we be more inclusive' tends to lead to different initiatives and outcomes compared to the questions and examples that you will find in this chapter. The next pages aim to inspire ideas as to how your business can empower individuals, communities, or regions across the world to contribute their best potential and tackle poverty and related issues at its root.

Not all empowerment initiatives have the desired outcomes, however. My research shows that some have significantly better results than others in terms of transforming people's lives, as well as commercial outcomes.

Let's look at a range of inspirational examples that empower people exceptionally well and uncover the key factors behind their success.

---

[38] Burns, 2013; Nussbaum, 2000; Sen 1999
[39] Burns, 2013; Haugh & Talwar, 2016

Empower like a genius

Michael Chance, a lovely young man with kind light blue eyes, tells me about how he lost his way in his late teens and was sent to prison for a year. Afterwards he came across an apprenticeship opportunity at Brigade and Beyond Food to become a chef.

Brigade and Beyond Food were founded by Simon Boyle, a passionate chef who began his career at The Savoy Hotel in London and was hand-picked by the Royal Academy of Culinary Arts to train at the top end of the hospitality market. After volunteering in Sri Lanka following the Tsunami in 2004, Simon wanted to do more for people struggling in his home country.

He first set up a food events company to provide opportunities to people from disadvantaged backgrounds. Like many other entrepreneurs trying to balance a commercial business with an impact purpose, he hit some tough challenges and learned some hard lessons.

After this experience, he set up the Brigade Bar and Bistro and the Beyond Food Foundation in partnership with PwC and Searcys.

Since opening in 2011, hundreds of people have transformed their lives through the training, accreditation, placements, and support they received.

At Brigade and Beyond Food, Michael Chance found something that he loved doing, and it transformed his life. After the apprenticeship, he landed a job in the prestigious Savoy Hotel in London.

Several other Brigade and Beyond Food apprentices told me how the opportunity had transformed their lives and of those around them. Like Sonya Blackwood, whose smile could not be bigger when she speaks about her apprenticeship. She explains: "What do my children think about me being here? They think it's great, they absolutely love it." Her facial expression becomes more serious and intense when she continues: "It just had a massive, huge positive knock-on effect throughout all of our lives."

My research shows that the success rate of getting people employed at Brigade and Beyond Food is 300-400% higher than other initiatives with a similar mission and context. At the same time, the business scores higher on commercial indicators such as revenue and profits. And the impact on people is much more transformational in terms of confidence, self-esteem, and overall improvement in quality of life.

So, why and how do Brigade and Beyond Food create far better outcomes than others? After comparing more and less successful examples systematically and analysing thousands of snippets of data, a strong pattern revealed what sets those with better results apart from others with lower success rates. They 'lead like a genius'.

As we saw earlier, Albert Rothenberg discovered a common trait that sets geniuses like Mozart, Einstein, and Da Vinci apart from other highly talented people. The critical difference they have in common is that geniuses "pursue the unity of opposites as part of a whole".

This is precisely what initiatives like Brigade and Beyond Food with high success rates do differently compared to others with a similar mission but with lower success rates. They do not pursue profits with a separate social or environmental purpose. At the same time, they do not lose sight of the profit goals of the business. Let's look at what this means in practice.

A common pitfall to avoid

The genius of Brigade and Beyond Food lies in pursuing profits and their mission to transform people's lives 'as part of a whole'. Many examples of even the most exemplary sustainable businesses in the world have had to learn this lesson the hard way.

The hard way is costly in using investment, time, and energy inefficiently, and ultimately leads to low-impact results. Moreover, it does not set the best example to others.

It is precisely the pitfall we fell into with our impact business in the Kibera slum in Nairobi. Our mission was to empower young women without an education with training and employment opportunities. From this perspective, it made sense that most of our workforce comprised of young women without an education. Based on our impact mission, selecting our recruits based on their need for an opportunity also made sense.

However, this approach caused enormous challenges considering our commercial reality, selling fashion across different parts of the world. We would have achieved a more robust financial platform by balancing our team better between highly skilled people and a small percentage of people who were not yet trained. And to select young women not just based on their need for the opportunity but also more strictly based on their potential and interest to become excellent tailors. This would have most likely ultimately empowered the young women better too.

Initiatives with superior outcomes than most like Brigade and Beyond Food avoid or overcome this pitfall. While their mission is to empower people, Brigade is an excellent restaurant, first and foremost. When we discuss the challenging balancing act between profits and purpose Simon Boyle asks: "Do you lead with the business, or do you lead with the mission and impact? I would say, each and every time, it has to be with the business. I have done it both ways. So, I can tell you, I have the scars to prove it. Ultimately, if the business isn't here, we can't help anybody anyway."

This means for example that Brigade and Beyond Food does not fill its kitchen only with apprentices as it aims to ensure excellent standards for the food it serves to its customers. So, the team consists of about 75% experienced chefs and 25% apprentices. Moreover, it does not select apprentices based solely on how much they need the opportunity. It recruits people based on their need for the opportunity and who, at the same time, have the potential and interest to be a great chef.

The apprentices are empowered more effectively by developing their potential as part of a successful business than an initiative that loses sight of the commercial objectives next to their impact mission.

Let's look at other empowerment examples in different contexts and see how the 'genius' in their leadership powers their success.

Apprentices at Brigade, London, UK

'GOOD profit' improves impact

Last year, I spoke to a lady who runs a back-to-work scheme in Scotland for mothers who had been out of work. I asked her: "Do you charge a recruitment fee to the companies that employ these women?".

She seemed surprised that I asked and explained that, like most similar initiatives, it does not charge for its service but relies on funding instead.

But, if the scheme leads to a good match between a candidate and a job opportunity, it seems fair for the agency's customers to pay for its services, so why would she not charge for its services like other recruitment companies? Or, if the initiative is not matching people well into suitable roles, then to what extent is it empowering people?

Initiatives that rely on funding instead of revenue often create a weak financial platform to sustain itself. An interesting finding from my research is that such models also achieve a lower success rate in getting people employed and who remain employed.

Let's compare this with Ctalents, a coaching and recruitment company in The Netherlands for people with a visual or hearing impairment, founded by Sandra Ballij. Ctalents does not just charge a fee for its services; it charges a bit more than other recruitment companies. And it can because of a strong focus on the value of their candidates to its clients. Ensuring high value means that employers often come back for more candidates.

Initiatives that rely on funding as opposed to paying customers can lack sufficient focus on aligning products and services with market needs. This often leads to a fragile financial platform to survive and grow. Moreover, by providing empowerment opportunities that are not well aligned with market demand, trainees tend to be less well equipped to find jobs beyond their training or apprenticeships.

This is not to say that funding does not have its place. Incentivising companies to empower people by funding the *additional* costs incurred – such as training costs or accessibility tools – is beneficial, but the core business model functions better when it relies on revenue. The drive to generate revenue strengthens the focus on aligning products or services with the market.

Ctalents is growing its revenue and impact each year at a steep rate. It empowers its candidates effectively by aligning their talents well with the right job opportunities. Like Brigade and Beyond Food, Ctalents achieves a 300-400% higher success rate of getting people into meaningful work compared to other similar initiatives. It has a far more profound transformative impact on people's lives regarding their confidence, self-esteem, improved relationships, quality of life, income, and prospects.

Sharon Veerbeek, a talented young woman, told me about her opportunity to work as a forensics consultant at PwC, coming through the Ctalents programme. A first thing that amazed me about Sharon is that despite being unable to hear anything, she had learned to speak two languages, English and Dutch. Sharon discusses the importance of not being seen as a 'victim'.

"I am very proud of how I have to prove myself," she says. They [PwC] don't pamper me. I still have to prove myself like everyone else."

Jeroen Govaard is First Waiter at Ctaste in Amsterdam, a restaurant where people can dine in the dark, served by waiters with visual impairments. Ctaste was also founded by Sandra Ballij, an entrepreneur with levels of enthusiasm that I have not seen in any other human.

The experience of eating in complete darkness is quite humbling. Much like ourselves, I could hear the other guests speaking softly, feeling some unease without being able to see anything at all, not even the contours of our surroundings. By contrast the waiters spoke and walked around fully confident, bringing it home how this is their normal.

Like Sharon, Jeroen emphasises the importance of empowerment.

"If you constantly treat somebody as blind, he will never go beyond that, and he will always feel blind and different," he explains. "I am convinced that is the same for people with all types of disabilities. It has really helped me that I wasn't treated with preconceived ideas about what I couldn't do but to have the opportunity to explore what you can do."

As Professor Yunus says, people, like bonsai trees, grow taller when given the right space. Jeroen and Sharon are prime examples of how people can flourish when they are given access to the right opportunities.

As a fraction of your business

Once we realise that empowerment tends to be more successful when it goes hand in hand with a solid commercial platform, we can see that mainstream companies are well placed to empower people out of poverty and social exclusion. To get started with empowerment, working with an organisation with the expertise to do this well can be helpful.

For example, the team at Ctalents guide organisations in ensuring proper accessibility requirements. Its expertise can also help to ensure that vacancies are aligned with people's talents. In this context, research shows that people with a visual or hearing impairment can develop other 'super-powers'. Brain imaging studies show that when one of the senses is deprived of input, the brain rewires itself to strengthen other senses, a phenomenon known as cross-modal neuroplasticity.[40]

By focusing on people's strengths, Ctalents has matched several candidates with a visual impairment with a career at the police to tap suspect conversations. Their ability to listen better compared to most others also proves to be an advantage in service-oriented roles such as mortgage advisors or marketing and communications. On the other hand, people with an audio impairment tend to have additional talents because of their enhanced eye for detail. This offers specific advantages in the role of analysts, image specialists, or forensics.

---

[40] Doucet, Guillemot, Lassonde, Gagné, Leclerc & Lepore, F., 2005; Karns, Dow & Neville, 2012; Nilsson & Schenkman, 2016; Sladen, Tharpe, Ashmead, Grantham & Chun, 2005

Transforming communities

Aside from providing training and employment, an organisation can locate its premises in areas that need economic development to empower people out of poverty – or it could opt to work with suppliers that do.

Goodwill Solutions in England provides logistics services to corporate clients such as Amazon and M&S. After a successful career in logistics Mike Britton, Founder of Goodwill Solutions, chose to locate its facilities near marginalised areas in Northampton to transform these communities. Its training and placement opportunities empower people with backgrounds ranging from care leavers, homelessness, ex-offenders and long-term unemployed, to gain work and better futures. Goodwill Solutions is very successful in doing so, with high success rates and transformative impact on people's lives, similar to Brigade and Beyond Food and Ctalents. It is also listed among Europe's FTSE fastest-growing companies.

When thinking outside of the box, business leaders can help to transform communities and regions. Globally, poverty rates are three times higher in rural areas compared to urban areas.[41] Considering that statistic, it seems worthwhile to think of creating training and employment opportunities aligned with a market need that could work well in poor, remote areas.

An inspirational example that does exactly that is Grassroutes, which has opened access to the travel industry in rural farming tribes in India such as Purushwadi. People in these communities typically live on less than $0.62 USD per day,[42] and many work as labourers on lands away from their children to make ends meet. The women I spoke to in Purushwadi, such as Vimal Kondar, told me about the hardship they faced, for example, when child labour posed problems while having challenges in accessing medical care. Many young people move away to city slums in search of work.

---

[41] UN, 2015a
[42] World Bank, 2020b

Vimal Kondar, Grassroutes, Purushwadi, India.

Grassroutes, founded by Inir Pinheiro and Uday Nanda, provides travellers with a unique experience of authentic India, away from typical tourist hotspots. It enables people to visit small farming communities while adhering to strong ethical standards and community ownership. Here, travellers get to see the 'real India' – how most people in India live. And taste genuinely authentic Indian food, cooked slowly on a wood fire.

By providing farmers with vital additional income, Grassroutes has freed parents from working for almost nothing on other people's lands away from their children. It has further enabled young people from the villages to remain or move back to the village. Duttraya Kondarv tells me full of joy how glad he is to have left the city slum in Mumbai and come back to the serene natural beauty of Purushwadi to work as a guide. Grassroutes estimates that their program has led to a reduction in migration to city slums of young people by 80% in the communities where they operate.

Can you think of creating similar opportunities in your industry? Or work with suppliers such as Goodwill Solutions or Grassroutes?

An example could be a tour operator including experiences offered by organisations such as Grassroutes in its tours. This would give travellers an unforgettable and authentic experience, while transforming people's lives and communities at the same time.

Empower through accessibility

Empowering people to use their talents aligned with market demand is an effective way to eradicate poverty and social exclusion.

However, as long as poverty and inequality exist, there is another way for companies to empower people. A strategy that can work well is multi-level pricing to make products and services accessible to people with different income levels. Aravind Eye Hospitals in India applies this solution to tackling blindness.

At least 4 million people in India develop cataracts – the primary cause of blindness – every year. Aravind has a reputation for excellence in eye care performing around 350,000 eye surgeries each year, making it the world's largest eyecare service.[43] About 40% of the operations are charged full price to those on high incomes. Sixty percent of the patients are either charged a low price or at no cost, depending on their income.[44]

The Grameen Bank is famous for making loans accessible to poor people in Bangladesh, who according to traditional banks were not 'loan worthy'. Providing micro-loans to mothers to support their businesses has lifted more than 9 million families out of poverty.[45]

There are criticisms of the micro-credit model and its limitations, some of which I will return to later. Nevertheless, by 2010, 68% of Grameen's millions of borrowers and their families had moved across the poverty line using indicators of having three meals a day, sleeping on a mattress instead of on the floor, and children going to school.[46]

---

[43] Wilcox, 2020
[44] Ramdas, 2022
[45] Garmeen Bank Annual Report, 2020
[46] Yunus, 2007; Yunus, Moingeon, & Lehmann-Ortega, 2010

Grameen and its founder, Professor Yunus, were awarded the Nobel Peace Prize in 2006 for developing the bank. Interestingly, they were awarded the Nobel Prize for *Peace* (as opposed to economics), recognising the importance of addressing poverty toward a more peaceful world.

A multi-tier pricing model at Grameen Bank makes its loans accessible to all. It adopts four different interest rates, charging the poorest members – those who are living on the streets – a 0% interest rate.[47]

In Scotland, comedian Janey Godley asks people at some gigs not to pay for tickets upfront but to deposit the money they can afford, and think is fair, in a bucket. She says: "Nobody should be too poor to see comedy. If you are skint, DO NOT put a penny in that bucket."[48]

Multi-tier pricing methods represent a useful model to make products and services affordable while enabling a profitable business model. However, like charitable support, these models do not tend to address the root cause of poverty and inequality as effectively as empowering people to make a good living by using their talents. But it can provide a sustainable intermediate solution until poverty and inequality have, as Professor Yunus coined during his interview, "been put into the museum".

---

[47] Grameen Bank, 2020
[48] Godley, 2019

It's good for business

When a company empowers people effectively, this can lead to substantial benefits. First, access to a broader pool of talented people is invaluable to most companies. But beyond that, there are other commercial advantages.

As we saw at the start of this book, there are the generic benefits of being a more impactful business such as better customer loyalty and referral rates – both of which underpin business growth. Other advantages include increased brand value, and productivity; but there are additional benefits to empowering people with your organisation.

A person who has been given an opportunity to flourish after being unable to do so tends to be very motivated. As Jeroen Govaard, First Waiter at Ctaste, says: "If you give someone who has been left out an opportunity to use their talents, you will see the benefits of a highly motivated team member, lower sick leave figures, and other interesting advantages."

Interestingly, such benefits tend to extend to the broader team. Sandra Ballij, Founder and CEO of Ctalents, explains how sick leave tends to reduce when a team recruits someone with a visual or hearing impairment. While it was never one of Ctalents' goals, it turns out that people are inspired by seeing their colleague with additional challenges showing up for work. Team members also feedback that it makes them feel more engaged, because they all feel more accepted for who they are.

Another advantage is the insight gained into a customer group with the same background as your recruits. Examples include people with a disability or those who have fled their home country. These insights can give companies a competitive edge by aligning their products and services more closely to the needs of this market segment.

If we look at the big picture, empowerment is only half of the answer to eradicating poverty, inequality, and related issues. In the next chapter we will look at the second part of the solution.

In a nutshell

1. Companies can help to eradicate poverty and social exclusion by empowering people to use their talents. By providing training and employment opportunities to those with a disadvantage, business leaders tackle the root cause of these global issues. This allows people and their families to transform their lives more structurally compared to a traditional 'giving back' approach.

2. Companies can transform communities by opening facilities in areas in need of economic development. Examples include Goodwill Solutions in Northampton, SoleRebels in more deprived regions in Ethiopia, or Grassroutes, which has enabled rural farming tribes in India to access the travel market.

3. Companies can focus on making their products and services more accessible by adopting, for example, a multi-tier pricing system. While this does not tackle the root cause of poverty, social exclusion, or inequality, it can provide a sustainable 'in-between' solution.

4. Organisations can benefit significantly by empowering people and communities, but most benefits only transpire when empowerment is well-balanced with a sound commercial model.

5. To tease out ideas for empowerment opportunities in the context of your organisation, you can use the questions summarised in the IMPACT Wheel on the opposite page.

Q1. Empowerment

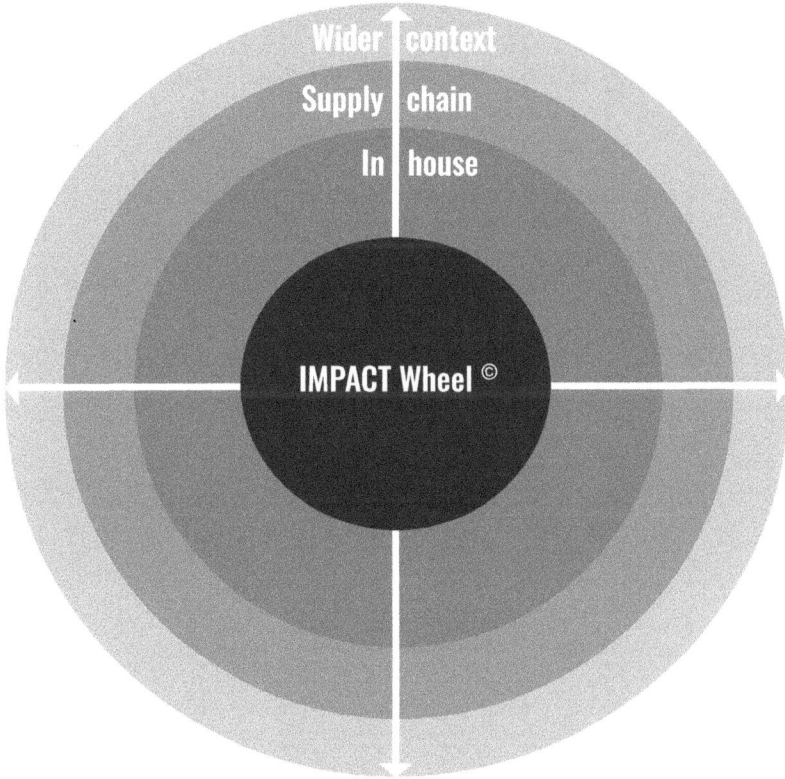

In house	Can you lift people out of poverty, social exclusion, and inequality by creating empowerment opportunities for:
	- Areas in need of economic development;
	- Refugees, young/ old long-term unemployed;
	- People with disabilities, or people from marginalised backgrounds?
Supply chain	Can you create empowerment opportunities in the supply chain? E.g., by procuring from certain suppliers, incentivising suppliers, or by making your products/ services more accessible?
Wider context	Can you inspire, educate, incentivise, or invest in others to create empowerment opportunities?

Chapter Three
Just Payments

Q2. Just Payments

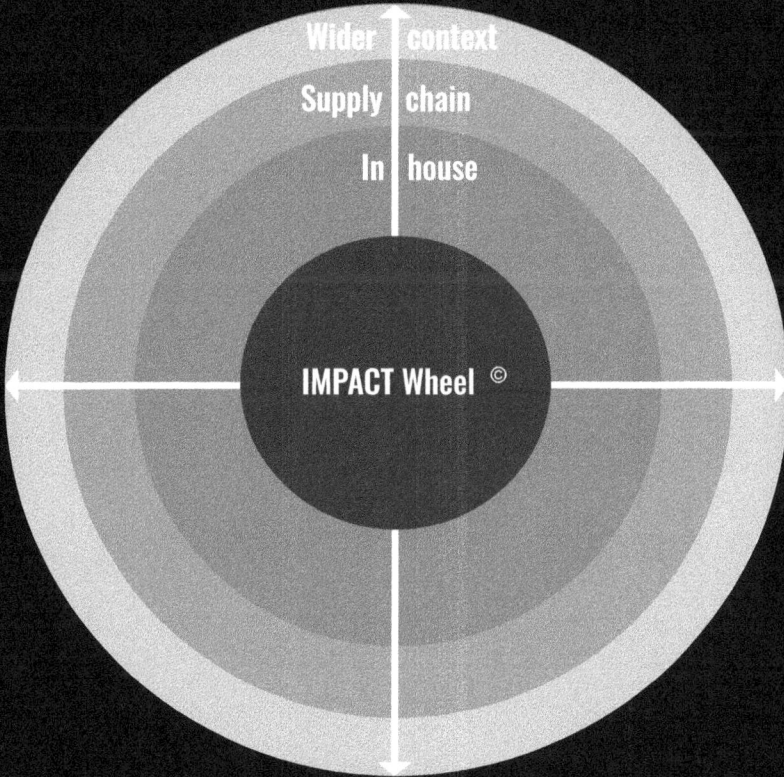

Wider | context

Supply | chain

In | house

IMPACT Wheel ©

> Like slavery and apartheid, poverty is not natural. It is man-made, and it can be overcome and eradicated by the action of human beings.

> Trade justice is a truly meaningful way to show commitment to bringing about an end to global poverty.

Nelson Mandela

Just Payments

Few philosophers would argue that everyone should earn the same. It works well to recognise different input levels for market incentives to work and resources to be allocated efficiently around market demand. Some people work harder, bring more talent, have more experience, and/or take more risk or initiative than others. But most economists agree that a well-functioning economic system should fairly reward contributions made.

The underlying notion of justice is "the constant and perpetual will to render to each his due", as defined by Roman Law in the sixth century CE.[49] The reality is that payments to different parties within companies and supply chains are increasingly no longer based on justice, 'to render each their due', but are based on positions of power instead. It is this injustice that for a large part has been and is feeding the rising inequality in almost all countries around the world.

Companies are well placed to change the course of history and counter the rising inequality by leading on 'Just Payments'. This is different from 'Fairtrade' or similar concepts that are based on setting a minimum price or minimum payment level. As the examples throughout this chapter show Just Payments means that payment levels reflect the level of contributions made by each of the actors within companies and across supply chains.

Interestingly, as the examples will show, those that are better at Just Payments can ultimately significantly outperform their competitors in terms of customer loyalty, sales and profit rates, revenue growth, earnings per share growth, and stock gains.

But first, as 'Just Payments' are often the least emphasised in sustainability discussions, let's discuss why this is so important for the future of humanity, before exploring examples and practical ways to implement it.

---

[49] Miller, 2017

We're boiling like frogs

In the fable of 'boiling a frog', the amphibian in a pot filled with pleasantly tepid water does not notice a gradual increase in heat and remains in the pot until it boils to death. Like the frog, we seem to be unaware of the gradually increasing inequality and related dangers. Leading scientists warn us that rising inequality is one of the biggest threats to our world.[50] President Obama, followed by the Economic World Forum, called inequality "the defining challenge of our time".[51]

From a global income inequality perspective, the richest 10% of the global population currently takes 52% of global income, whereas the poorest half of the population earns 8.5% of it.[52] Wealth inequalities are even more pronounced with the poorest half of the global population owning just 2% of the total and the richest 10% possessing 76% of all wealth.[53]

At a national level inequality has grown rapidly since 1980 within almost all countries.[54] The World Inequality Report highlights that over the last two decades the gap between the average incomes of the top 10% and the bottom 50% of individuals within countries has almost doubled.[55] In the US, 17% of children live below the poverty line.[56] Food banks in the Trussell Trust's UK wide network distributed 2.9 million emergency food parcels to people facing hardship in 2022, more than double compared to five years before, with more than one million of these parcels distributed for children.[57] When I grew up in The Netherlands, food banks and homelessness were uncommon. This is sadly no longer the case.

---

[50] Chancel et al., 2022; Chang, 2010; Piketty, 2014; Piketty, 2020; Stiglitz, 2013
[51] Obama, 2013
[52] Chancel et al., 2022
[53] Chancel et al., 2022
[54] Alvaredo et al., 2018; Chancel et al., 2022; Piketty, 2015; World Inequality Database, 2020
[55] Chancel et al., 2022
[56] US Census Bureau, 2022
[57] Russel Trust, 2023

If we take the US and the UK as examples of high inequality, we can increasingly see the cracks in our societies as a result. Professor Joseph Stiglitz, former Chief Economist at the World Bank and Nobel Prize Laureate, predicts that countries like the US and the UK are approaching the level of inequality of countries such as Iran, Jamaica, and Uganda, facing significant social and economic consequences by 2050.[58] Most other countries do not have the same level of inequality yet but are heading in the same direction.

Studies show us that inequality adversely impacts crime rates, life expectancy, economic growth, suicide rates, and the physical and mental health not just of those on the unfortunate end of inequality, but of all people in society.[59] Moreover, inequality undermines the social fabric in our societies, leading to division, polarisation, the rise of populism, extremism, increased tensions, social unrest, instability, and conflicts.[60]

Looking at the US Biden vs. Trump election or the UK Brexit referendum, we can indeed see two unequal, highly divided countries. Extremism and populism are on the rise across many countries. Shoplifting has increased steeply in both the US and UK. Over the past couple of years, more and more cab drivers here in Glasgow will only take customers if they in pay cash. Studies show that both the US and the UK have experienced a rise of depression, self-harm, and suicide among 15-to-24-year-olds, associated with the level of income inequality.[61] It is scary to think of how our societies will develop over the next few decades if we do not manage to curb the inequality trends.

---

[58] Stiglitz, 2013
[59] Enamorado, López-Calva, Rodríguez-Castelán & Winkler, 2014; McAuley, 2007; McCall, 2016; McCarty, OECD, 2016; Piketty, 2020; Stiglitz, 2013; UN, 2023; Wilkinson and Pickett, 2009
[60] Stiglitz, 2013; UN, 2015b
[61] Twenge et al., 2019; Padmanathan et al., 2020

A dangerously misleading picture

At this point, it is worth going off on a brief tangent. When I show poverty statistics during talks, some participants refer to *Factfulness* by Rosling et al. Their perception from this book is that 'poverty is not that bad anymore'. The first time I heard this, I was surprised. Seriously? How can it be 'not so bad' that more than half of everyone in our world struggles to meet basic needs? The statistics I use are based on sources widely regarded as reliable, such as the World Bank, UN, OECD, or Oxford's OurWorldInData. Rosling uses the same sources. So, how could people come to that conclusion? When I read the book, I realised why.

The main graph used in *Factfulness*[62] (see below) and other statistics in the book refer to income levels based on a *country's average*. Rosling writes: "Today, most people, 75%, live in middle-income countries", and "only 9% of the world lives in low-income countries". But herein lies the potential for a dangerous misrepresentation of reality.

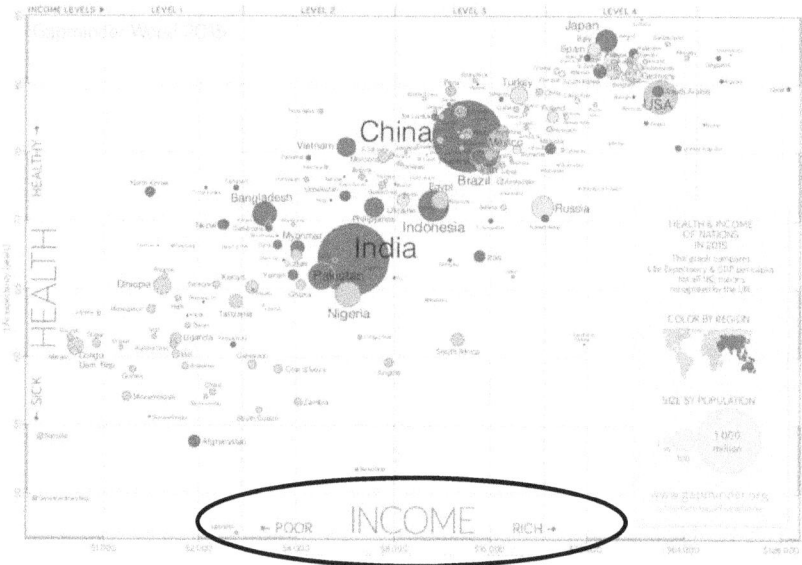

[62] *Factfulness*, Rosling et al., gapminder.com, permission to use, cc-by license

Let's consider this using India as an example. Rosling portrays India as a large bubble around a 'middle-income' level. Now, let's check the reality of the income of more than 1.3 billion people in India instead of the country's average. The black bubbles I added to the graph below show how many people in India live on each income level[63] (excluding 'health' on the y-axis). Income levels on the left reflect extreme poverty and wealthy incomes on the right.

As the reality of the millions of people in the black bubbles shows, placing a country bubble like India in 'level two' based on the country's *average* income is a rather misleading picture. The *average* income of the 1.4 billion people in India might be on level two. That does not mean that all these people no longer live in extreme poverty. In fact, the latest estimates by the World Bank are that despite all the significant progress, more than half of the population in India, 750 million people, still have to get by on less than $3.20 USD per day.[64]

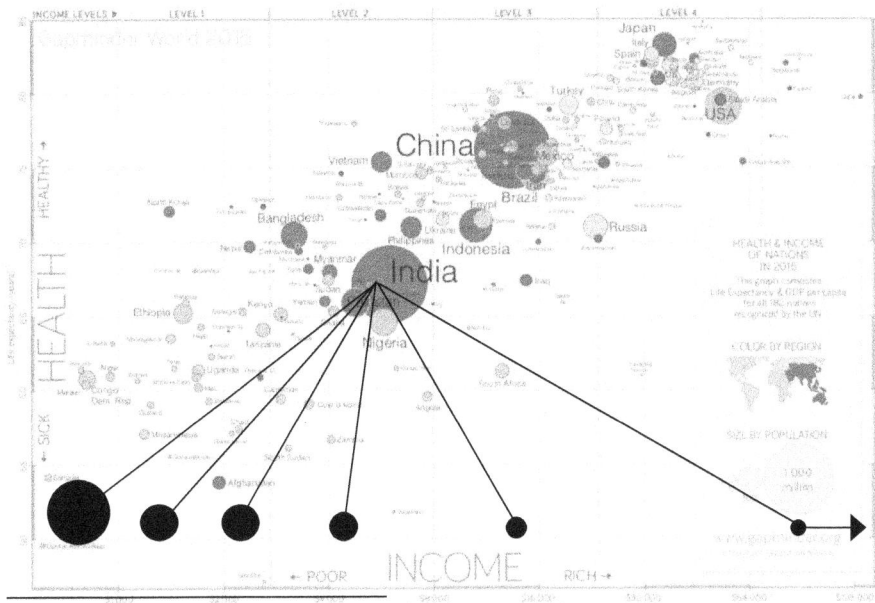

---

[63] World Bank, 2020b; Statista 2020; Graph adjusted based on free material from gapminder.com, permission to use, cc-by license.
[64] World Bank, 2020b

Of those 750 million people, 270 million live below the national poverty line, which means less than $0.72 USD per day. These people live below a third of the international measure of extreme poverty. This number of people alone is around 27 times the whole population of Sweden. These were the poverty figures before Covid-19. Like the global predictions, the pandemic is expected to have increased poverty in India significantly.[65]

Can you imagine living on less than $3.20 USD daily like the 750 million people in India? Or worse, living on less than $0.72 USD a day like the 270 million people in India who do? I was mortified when I saw that the graph had clustered all these people into a 'middle-income bubble'.

Rosling makes an excellent point that the perception of countries traditionally seen as 'developing' is entirely outdated. Many people in these countries are as wealthy and some far richer than people in countries that were traditionally seen as 'developed'. But when Rosling writes that 75% of the global population lives in middle-income countries, this does not mean that *all people* in these countries have a middle income. If a country is middle-income on average *and* at the same time has low inequality, like Rosling's home country of Sweden, then yes, this means most of the people in that country have a good income.

The critical difference with Rosling's home country is that most of the world's countries have a much higher level of inequality. Sweden has long been known as one of the most equal countries in the world, with a Gini index of 0.28 (with 0 representing perfect equality and 1.0 representing perfect inequality).[66] It is quite the opposite in India: while India is one of the fastest-growing economies in the world, it is also one of the most unequal countries, with a rising Gini index of 0.50.[67]

---

[65] World Bank, 2020b
[66] OECD, 2020
[67] OECD, 2020

This does not just apply to India. The countries with the largest populations in our world (China, India, the US, Indonesia, Pakistan, Brazil, and Nigeria), together making up half the global population, each show high inequality.[68] If we would split these countries into bubbles according to actual income levels, Rosling's income graph would show a very different picture, more accurately reflecting the different income levels across our world.

I do not believe that Rosling wanted to convey that 'poverty is no longer that bad'. On the contrary, he writes: "The Five Global Risks We *Should* Worry About include extreme poverty, climate change, world war, financial collapse, and a global pandemic."[69] Well, he was not wrong on the latter.

Rosling adds: "Be less stressed by the imaginary problems of an overdramatic world and more alert to the real problems and how to solve them."[70] He emphasises the importance of resolving poverty, not only to alleviate the misery of people living it, but to help prevent civil wars, terrorism, and outbreaks of pandemics with no health services to respond to them at an early stage.

While poverty gets much attention in *Factfulness*, inequality does not, even though many studies and prominent experts highlight the dangers of the rising inequality, more so compared to poverty itself. These experts include Joseph Stiglitz, economist and Professor at Columbia University, Nobel Prize winner and former Chief Economist at the World Bank; Thomas Piketty, Professor at the Paris School of Economics; and Ha-Joon Chang, Professor of Development Economics at the University of Cambridge.

So, how can we counteract rising inequality, to create more flourishing societies? Knowing that the upward trend is primarily caused by the rapid increase in income inequality,[71] we realise that companies are very well-placed to help tackle this.

---

[68] OECD, 2020
[69] Rosling, 2018, pp. 237 to 241
[70] Rosling, 2018, pp. 237 to 241
[71] Piketty, 2014; Stiglitz, 2013

Have workers become 1900% less productive?

Wage inequalities have exploded since the 1980s in the US in particular, but also in most other countries.[72] To understand how unjust payments have become, we can look at the CEO-to-average worker pay gap increase over the past four decades. This gap has risen by 1,900% in the US, with a ratio of 20:1 in 1965 to around 400:1 in 2021.[73] This includes salary and other benefits such as bonuses and pensions.

Based on analysing benchmark stock indexes in 22 nations, a Bloomberg study found the following five countries to show the largest CEO-to-average worker pay gaps:

1. The US,
2. India,
3. The United Kingdom,
4. South Africa, and
5. The Netherlands.

The study indicates that countries like Sweden and Japan, by comparison, have an around 1,000% lower pay gap ratio.[74]

---

[72] Bloomberg, 2018; Chang, 2010; Economic Policy Institute, 2020; Institute for Policy Studies, 2019; Piketty, 2014; Stiglitz, 2013

[73] Bloomberg, 2018; Economic Policy Institute, 2020; Institute for Policy Studies, 2019

[74] Bloomberg, 2018

The ratios beg essential questions. Have CEOs in the US started contributing 1,900% more in recent decades? Or has the input by the average worker gone down by 1,900%? Do workers in the US, UK, India, and The Netherlands contribute 1,000% relatively less than their peers in Sweden or Japan?

Research by both Stiglitz, Nobel Prize Laureate and previous Chief Economist at the World Bank, and Piketty, Professor at the Paris School of Economics, shows that the increasing gap in wages is one of the major causes of the rise in inequality, next to increasing disparities in wealth, with 'trickle-down economics' (the theory that in an economic system in which the poorest gradually benefit as a result of the increasing wealth of the richest) proven to be a myth.[75]

Over the past two decades the gap between the average incomes of the top 10% and the bottom 50% of individuals within countries has almost doubled.[76] In three decades the income of the 0.1% highest earners in the US has increased by more than 300%, for the 1% highest earners it has risen by 150%, while those with higher education have seen their income decline by 10% over the same period, and the income of families with parents who graduated from high school have had a reduction by more than 25%.[77]

---

[75] Chang, 2010; Piketty, 2014; Stiglitz, 2013
[76] Chancel et al., 2022
[77] Stiglitz, 2013

While the US has always portrayed itself as the land of equal opportunity, Stiglitz shows that the chances of making it from a bottom income level to the top are slim.[78] There are always exceptions, but the statistics show that only 8% of children from poor backgrounds make it to a high-level income.[79] Economists show that this poverty trap does not just relate to parental income and education but already starts in the uterus due to exposure to different nutrition and pollution, with lifelong effects.[80]

We seem to be sleepwalking into the detrimental consequences of the rising income gap on our world. With a trend that is expected to keep growing, we can expect crime rates, social unrest, and our physical and mental health to worsen a lot more – not to mention the increasing polarisation of our societies, a perfect breeding ground for populism, radicalisation, and extremism.

Questions can be raised about the validity of reasons behind the rising pay gaps. While it is not a like-for-like comparison due to their different sizes, an observation of Costco versus Walmart provides interesting insights.

---

[78] Stiglitz, 2013
[79] Stiglitz, 2013
[80] Bowles, Durlauf & Hoff, 2006; Burns, 2013; Currie, 2011

Costco vs Walmart

Costco is a warehouse-style retailer based in the US, with annual revenues of more than $100 billion USD. Costco is known for offering relatively low C-suite salaries but higher pay for average workers, with 50% of its workforce earning more than $25 USD per hour.

When the average US public company CEO earned a salary of $14.2 million USD in 2012, Costco awarded its Co-Founder and former CEO Jim Senegal a salary of $350,000 USD in the same year. While CEO remuneration has increased since Senegal left as CEO, the pay gap in Costco remains far lower than its competitors. In 2020, the total CEO remuneration at Walmart was $22 million USD. At Costco, it was $8 million USD. The pay gap between Costco's CEO and the starting wage was almost 400% less than Walmart's.

The argument to increase remuneration at the top (and less at the bottom) is often that this is needed to attract talented leaders who are better able to improve a company's performance. Based on this logic you would expect Walmart to significantly outperform Costco.

Interestingly, Costco's annualised revenue growth of 6.3% from 2014 to 2019 is nearly four times Walmart's growth rate of 1.6% during those years. Also, Costco's annualised earnings per share growth during the same period at 12% was much higher than Walmart's at minus 14%.[81] Over the past five years Costco's stock has grown 880% with 20 times increase in margins and nearly 60% compounded revenue growth over five years – more than Apple, Amazon, and Google.[82]

Costco's impressive performance can partly be explained by its employees achieving far better sales and profit rates, with happier staff resulting in

---

[81] Forbes, 2020
[82] Brewer, 2023

more satisfied customers.[83] For most companies, customer loyalty and referrals are vital contributors to growth. Costco is famous for its customer loyalty. Its customer membership renewal rate hits around 85% to 90% each year[84]. In 2023 it reached 92.5%.[85] Staff at Costco stay an average of nine years at the company – at Walmart, they leave within three years on average.[86]

Organisations like Mondragón in Spain and the John Lewis Partnership in the UK lead on Just Payments by adopting employee ownership models. The John Lewis Partnership, a retailer in the UK for almost a century, has more than 90,000 staff – called partners – in the business, enabling employees to purchase five-year bonds in return for an annual 4.5% dividend plus shop vouchers.[87] Most of the 70,000 employees at Mondragón are partners of the collection of 96 enterprises, meaning that they own the companies.[88]

'Steward ownership' is a similar model adopted by a growing number of companies including Patagonia, Bosch, Zeiss, Rolex, and Carlsberg. Steward-owned companies have no outside shareholders, but voting shares are managed by 'stewards', such as employees or trustees, – people whose role is to serve the mission and continuity of the company.

Dutch telecom provider Voys recently adopted the steward ownership model, instead of selling its shares externally. Mark Vletter, Founder of Voys, comments that the model feels fair to him: "I didn't build the business, the 250 staff have, and we have been able to rely on support by the Dutch infrastructure." Vletter explains that he opted for steward ownership as he wants to ensure that Voys remains focused on creating value for society.[89]

---

[83] Sisodia et al., 2014
[84] Costco Annual Report, 2022; Forbes, 2016
[85] Brewer, 2023; Kiedrowski, 2023
[86] Comparably, 2023
[87] John Lewis, 2011; Raworth, 2017
[88] WEAll, 2023
[89] Swiers, 2023

How It Should Be

In many supply chains, one player holds most of the power. Across Europe, supermarkets represent a prime example. Under EU law, power is not objectionable *per se* but abusing such power is unlawful. Such abuse can lead to unjust prices, fees that barely cover producers' costs, late payments impacting their cash flow or sudden unexpected costs by demanding unforeseen discounts. As a result of such practices, suppliers across Europe have been forced out of business or survived on shallow profit margins. Small and medium enterprises (SMEs) in the food sector and farmers have been made especially vulnerable.[90]

An example is the average farm gate milk price paid to dairy farmers in the UK. Between 2016 and 2023 the average farm gate milk price has increased from 27 pence to 34 pence per litre.[91] The average cost of production has increased from around 25 pence per litre in 2016 to an estimated 40 pence per litre in 2022, meaning that many farmers have been struggling to cover their production costs.[92]

Let's compare this to HISBE, a self-styled 'rebel' supermarket based in Brighton in the UK. For every British pound spent in its supermarket, HISBE pays its suppliers 67 pence – a significantly higher rate compared to most large supermarkets. This has important knock-on effects, enabling farmers to pay their staff a fair wage and keep their animals in better welfare conditions. As HISBE's name says, it is 'How It Should Be'. This is an excellent example of Just Payments, where the slices of the pie are distributed more in proportion to each party's input. While HISBE pays its suppliers a significantly higher share than traditional supermarkets, it has a gross profit margin of 32%.

---

[90] Jack, 2021; Nicholson & Young, 2012; Partridge & Butler, 2023
[91] AHDB, 2020; AHDB, 2023; EFRAC, 2016; Partridge & Butler, 2023
[92] EFRAC, 2016; Horne, 2022

Wealth creation has merit if it reflects the value created and all parties involved are paid 'their fair dues'. But, a distributor who takes too much of the proportion of the jointly created wealth across the supply chain is not becoming wealthy by creating its share but by taking a share of the wealth that rightfully belongs to others. In the words of US economist Joseph Stiglitz, "there are two ways to become wealthy, to create wealth, or to take wealth away from others".[93]

We see the injustice in how payments are divided across supply chains in many sectors with the smallest share often going to the actual creators: the farmers, the producers, and the creatives. Should dairy farmers in the UK struggle to break even based on the prices they are forced to accept by supermarkets that hold the power in their supply chain?[94] Is it just that pineapple and banana farmers in Costa Rica who grow and harvest the fruits that we eat get paid 4% of the price that we pay compared to 29%-41% of the price going to the retailer? Is it fair that almost all authors make a loss on the books that they spent years of their lives writing?

Björn Ulvaeus, singer and songwriter of ABBA and co-producer of the film *Mamma Mia!* is trying to bring attention to the imbalance in the music industry. During an interview with Sky News he explains that "The core of the music industry for me has always been the song but somehow the songwriters have always been regarded as something on the periphery rather than the star of the whole thing"[95]. Ulvaeus continues: "I think that more and more people realise that the ecosystem is dysfunctional. It needs to be so that no party is unhappy. And as it is right now, more and more songwriters have to drive Ubers because of the imbalance."

---

[93] Stiglitz, 2013
[94] AHDB, 2020; EFRAC, 2016; Jack, 2021; Partridge & Butler, 2023
[95] Sky News, 2021

Just Payments transform lives

Tony's Chocolonely's story began in 2002 when Teun van de Keuken, a Dutch investigative reporter, travelled to the cocoa plantations in Ghana to report on child labour. Most of the world's cocoa is produced in Ghana and the Ivory Coast.[96] Children working on the cocoa farms have been in the media spotlight for working in adverse conditions and child trafficking.[97] Globally, 160 million children are engaged in child labour, with 79 million being exposed to its worst forms, including all forms of slavery, sale, and trafficking, forced labour, and child prostitution.[98]

A study at the University of Chicago shows that on average 43% of children living in agricultural households in cocoa growing areas age 5 to 17 are engaged in hazardous child labour in cocoa production.[99] The majority of these children are between age 5 to 11.[100]

When Teun witnessed the child labour during his investigative trip to the plantations he was so shocked, that he decided to record himself eating chocolate and took himself to court for 'knowingly purchasing an illegally manufactured product'. He asked four former child labour victims to back his case and testify against him. The Dutch attorney general dismissed the case for being outside its jurisdiction.

When none of the chocolate manufacturers he contacted showed any interest in producing chocolate bars differently, Teun started manufacturing his own chocolate in 2006. Now, 17 years later, the chocolate manufacturer Tony's Chocolonely has grown rapidly into a successful global brand.

---

[96] Nkamleu & Kielland, 2006
[97] Edmonds & Schady, 2012; Nelson & Phillips, 2018; Noble, 2017
[98] ILO, 2020
[99] NORC, 2020
[100] NORC, 2020

The root cause of child and illegal labour in the cocoa sector is poverty.[101] To address this Tony's Chocolonely pays between 22% and 61% over the farm gate price. In addition, it proactively monitors for illegal child labour.

Henk-Jan Beltman, who took over as CEO at Tony's Chocolonely in 2010, tells me passionately how its pricing impacts the lives of families in West Africa. He says: "Today, you cannot be proud of eating chocolate. Around 60% of all the cocoa comes from farmers in Western Africa. There are 1.6 million children working on these farms. We have long-term relationships directly with farmers and their cooperatives, and we pay a better farm gate price for a long period, and the impact on that is huge."

The government's farm gate price for the main and mid-crop seasons is so low that the farmers and their families live in poverty. Fairtrade premiums on top of the farm gate price are insufficient to earn a living income. The prices Tony's Chocolonely pays are higher than Fairtrade prices and are based on a living income, the net annual income a household needs to afford a decent standard of living for all its members.

Through Tony's Chocolonely's progressive pricing policy, 55% to 61% of the families in the communities where it sources cocoa, have been lifted out of poverty.[102]

Beyond that, Tony's Chocolonely aims to raise awareness of the ongoing low prices that are paid by other chocolate brands to the plantations; prices that perpetuate poverty, inequality, and child labour; prices that do not reflect the contribution made by the farmers to the chocolate that we eat.

In a world of Just Payments, prices would not only be based on minimum standards. With the underlying principle of justice to 'render each their due', prices would reflect the level of contribution made by each party across the supply chain.

---

[101] Cho, Fang, Tayur, & Xu, 2017
[102] NORC Report, 2020

Tony's Chocolonely headquarters in Amsterdam, The Netherlands

Amplifying Just Payments

Companies can tackle the root cause of poverty and inequality by applying Just Payments, firstly 'in house' and secondly, across their supply chain. The third circle of the IMPACT Wheel illustrates a third impact opportunity area by amplifying 'Just Payments' in a wider context.

Tony's Chocolonely's mission is not just to end illegal labour and exploitation on the cocoa plantations it buys from. It aims to inspire the wider chocolate sector to change their practices and runs campaigns to increase awareness of the issues on the plantations in West Africa. Henk-Jan Beltman, previous Chief Chocolate Officer at Tony's Chocolonely, explains during our interview: "We're working together to make the chocolate world free from child labour. That's our vision. And that goes further than our own chocolate; that's all chocolate worldwide.

"So, if you want 100% chocolate without child labour, communicate the problem, be an example, and inspire to make sure the big guys take responsibility to act in a similar way."

Triodos Investment Management provides another example of how to encourage Just Payments toward tackling inequality in a wider context. It aims to create awareness and transparency around the widening pay gaps and consequences. The bank has started an initiative to engage with some of the largest listed companies with excessive pay gap ratios through regular discussions, with a lack of progress potentially leading to divestment.[103]

If we empower people to contribute their potential and Just Payments become the new norm, we can 'close the tap' of much of our world's poverty and inequality-related issues. There would be much less need to deal with the symptoms and compensate for the injustices.

By 'pre-distributing' income based on justice, we would fix poverty and inequality in a more effective and dignified way than with 'redistribution' through welfare or charitable donations as an aftermath.

---

[103] Triodos, 2022

In a nutshell

1. Inequality is rising in most countries, with scary consequences, including polarisation of our societies, increased social unrest, crime rates, suicide rates, and a decline in our physical and mental health.

2. Beware of the country income averages in *Factfulness*; these can lead to the wrong perception of poverty and inequality. More than half of our global population is struggling to meet basic needs on less than $6.85 USD per day.[104] It's estimated that 700 million people live in extreme poverty on less than $2.15 USD per day.[105]

3. Not many economists suggest everyone should earn the same, but most agree it should be based on justice. The definition of justice is to 'pay each party their due', reflecting each party's contribution. In many companies and supply chains, pricing is not based on justice but on power, contributing to the explosion of income inequalities since 1980.

4. Business leaders can offer structural solutions to curb inequality by implementing Just Payments (different from 'Fairtrade' or similar concepts with minimum pricing or payment levels), using the questions on the next page.

---

[104] World Bank, 2022b
[105] World Bank, 2022a

Q2. Just payments

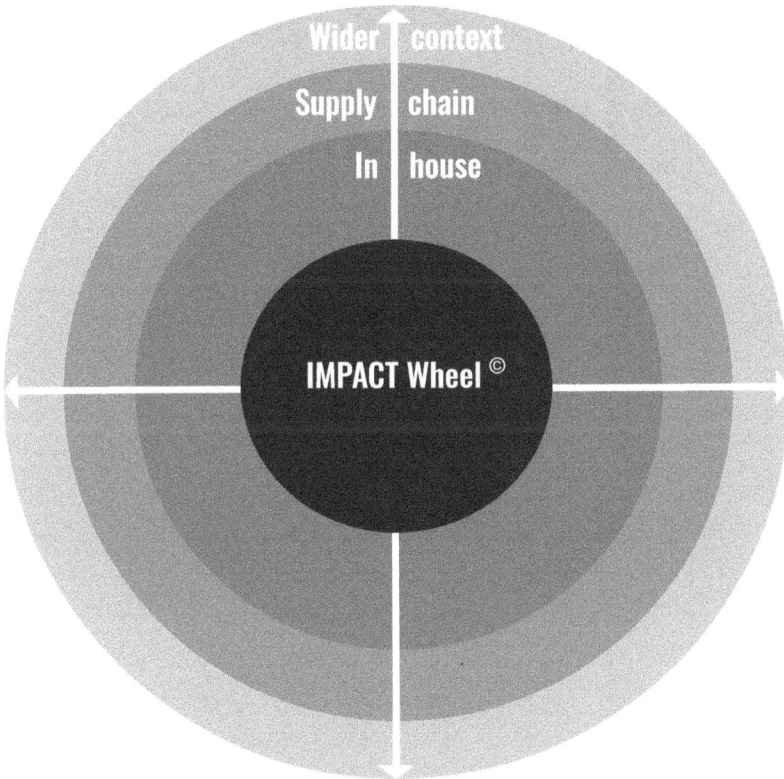

Wider | context
Supply | chain
In | house

IMPACT Wheel ©

In house   Can you divide income across your teams more justly, reflecting the contribution made by each party? For example, by lowering the CEO-to-average-worker pay gap, or by employee ownership schemes.

Supply chain Can you create Just Payment initiatives across your supply chain to reflect the contributions made by each party to tackle the root cause of poverty, inequality, and child labour?

Wider context Can you inspire, educate, incentivise and/or invest in others to create Just Payment opportunities in a wider context?

Chapter Four
Planet

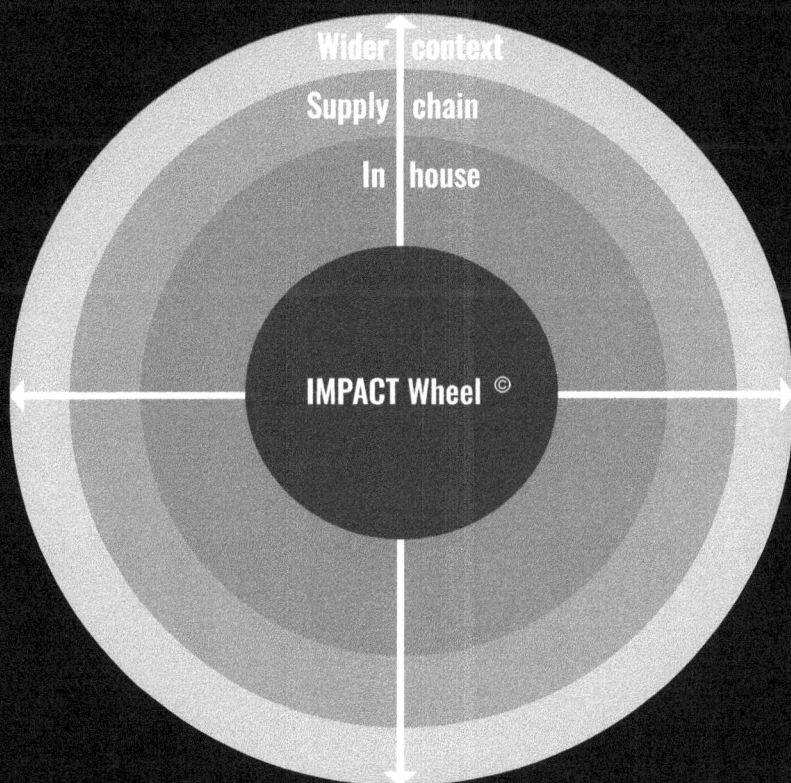

Wider context
Supply chain
In house

IMPACT Wheel ©

Q3. Planet

When I ask workshop participants how much the aviation industry contributes to global greenhouse gas emissions, most people estimate it at between 10% and 50%. In reality, the aviation industry contributes around 2% to greenhouse gas emissions, with energy use in industry and buildings representing the most significant contributors at 24.2% and 17.5% respectively.[106]

The media often points at flying as one of the major ways to cut carbon emissions. I have read articles with misleading figures that project the percentage contribution of this sector to be much larger in the future but with calculations that only consider the growth of aviation while ignoring growth in other sectors. If we look at data from Climate Watch and the World Resources Institute,[107] we see that since 1990, the fastest-growing sources of greenhouse gas emissions are:

1. Industrial processes (203% growth).
2. Electricity and heating (84% growth).
3. Transportation (78% growth, road transport the main contributor).

Aviation may be accused disproportionately to its actual contribution because flight-related emissions are fairly easy to measure. It is much harder to measure the footprint of a person or an organisation in terms of the full lifecycle of the products and services we buy. To account for this accurately means considering all related emissions, such as sourcing raw materials and resources, production, distribution, packaging and waste across supply chains, emissions related to all staff involved, and the buildings used. Much less straightforward.

I am not suggesting that airlines should not make improvements. But if we look at the chart on the opposite page, we see that some of the most significant opportunities to cut emissions are energy use in buildings and industry.

---

[106] OurWorldInData, 2023.
[107] Climate Watch, 2023; The World Resources Institute, 2023

Global Greenhouse Gas Emissions [108]

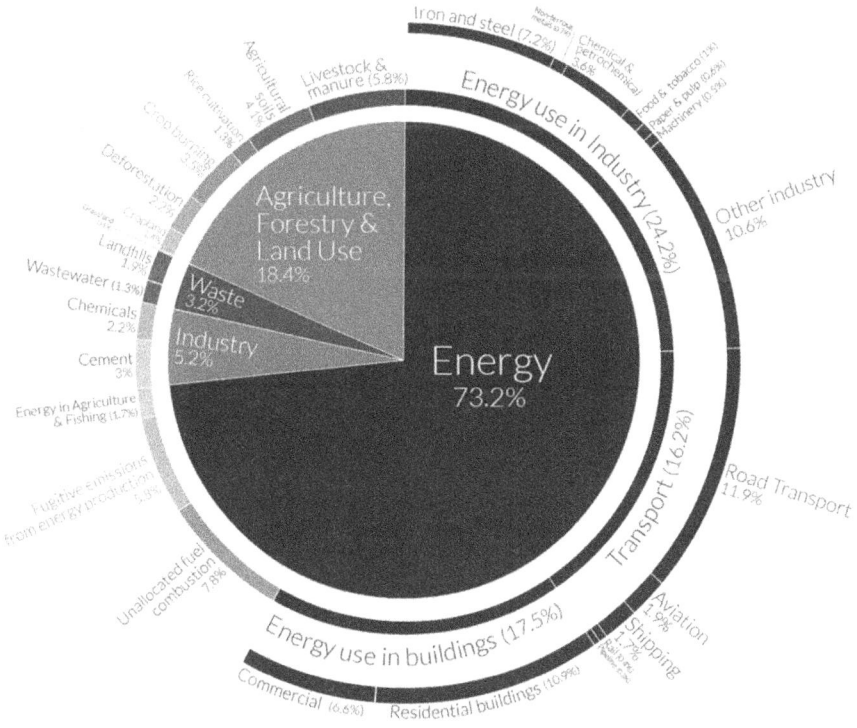

Iron and steel (7.2%) | Non-ferrous metals (0.7%) | Chemical & petrochemical 3.6% | Food & tobacco (1%) | Paper & pulp (0.6%) | Machinery (0.5%)

Agricultural Soils 4.1%
Rice cultivation 1.3%
Livestock & manure (5.8%)
Crop burning 3.5%
Deforestation 2.2%
Cropland 1.4%
Landfills 1.9%
Wastewater (1.3%)
Chemicals 2.2%
Cement 3%
Energy in Agriculture & Fishing (1.7%)
Fugitive emissions from energy production 5.8%
Unallocated fuel combustion 7.8%

Agriculture, Forestry & Land Use 18.4%
Waste 3.2%
Industry 5.2%
Energy 73.2%

Energy use in Industry (24.2%)
Other industry 10.6%

Transport (16.2%)
Road Transport 11.9%
Aviation 1.9%
Shipping 1.7%
Rail 0.4%
Pipeline 0.3%

Energy use in buildings (17.5%)
Commercial (6.6%)
Residential buildings (10.9%)

---

[108] OurWorldInData, 2023

To understand where we can invest our time and effort most effectively, it is vital to understand how business relates to climate change and its related issues. And it is important to be aware of the other major issues that are threatening an environment in which we as humanity can thrive.

A few months before this book is going to print, the UN Global Stocktake reports that the world is far from meeting the Paris agreement to limit warming to below 2 degrees Celsius and ideally to 1.5 degrees.[109]

Earth's temperature has already risen by at least 1.1 degrees since the pre-industrial period.[110] Extreme weather, such as heatwaves, floods, droughts, and storms, has tripled since 1960.[111] An estimated 60,000 additional annual deaths are expected due to the increase in extreme weather events, and a further 250,000 annual deaths due to heat stress, particularly for those with cardiovascular conditions or respiratory disease, as well as an increase in climate-related diseases such as malaria.[112]

Average sea levels have risen by 19cm since 1900 and are predicted to rise 40-63cm by 2100. With oceans absorbing 30% of carbon dioxide, acidity levels have increased by 26% since the industrial revolution, leading to a decline of coral reefs by 70-90% at 1.5 degrees warming and a daunting 99% at two degrees.[113]

---

[109] UN Global Stocktake, 2023
[110] UN Global Stocktake, 2023
[111] WHO, 2018
[112] WHO, 2018
[113] IPPC, 2018

The risk of irreversible loss of many ecosystems increases with the extent of global warming, especially at 2 degrees or more. The Living Planet Index shows that there has been an average decline of 69% across 31,821 studied animal populations of 5,230 species in our world from 1970 to 2018.[114]

Water pollution and increased water scarcity affects more than 40% of our global population. Air pollution is estimated to cause 6.5 million deaths annually[115] (more than double the global annual deaths caused by Covid-19 during the first two years of the pandemic).[116]

If the current trend continues, there will be more plastic in our oceans than fish by 2050 (by weight) unless we drastically change things around.[117] The growing plastics crisis is already having severe impacts on biodiversity as well as our health, with micro-plastics having entered our food chain, the water that we drink, and the air that we breathe.

---

[114] WWF, 2022
[115] OECD/IEA, 2016
[116] OurWorldInData, 2020b
[117] Ellen McArthur Foundation, 2022

Let's look at examples of organisations that tackle climate change and other environmental issues more and less effectively. Those that tackle the root cause as opposed to the symptoms of pollution and harmful emissions. We will look at ways to apply upstream instead of downstream solutions towards a circular economy, meaning an economy where waste and pollution is eliminated.[118]

We will see the importance of considering the whole system around the products and services we use. We will unravel key factors that underpin the most successful outcomes in genuinely reducing emissions and other harm to our planet. And we will investigate innovative solutions that can significantly improve how we impact our world and create good business benefits simultaneously.

At this point, it is worth noting that business leaders from service-oriented sectors sometimes wonder how specific solutions that appear to be more related to manufacturing apply to them. You may be surprised at how using the concepts that will follow can lead to a powerful impact in other contexts.

---

[118] OECD, 2022

Leading the way to Net Zero

The documentary film *Beyond Zero* features the story of the global sustainability leader Interface Inc. Its journey to go beyond net zero began in 1994 when customers asked the carpet tile manufacturer what it was doing for the environment.

"…We had no answers," recalls Interface's Founder Ray Anderson. "It was very embarrassing. And awkward for our sales, manufacturing, and research people."[119]

The interest by customers sparked Anderson's interest, and a strong passion to really change things took hold when he read *The Ecology of Commerce*[120] by environmentalist and economist Paul Hawken. The book gave Ray a better understanding of how his business was impacting Earth. He recalls how reading it hit him "like a spear in the chest".

In 1994, Interface embarked on a mission to achieve net zero by 2020; a mission that, at the time, seemed outrageous for a large multinational in a sector with traditionally high emissions and pollution. Anderson credits the bold mission as a key factor for sparking the fire instilled in the organisation's original sustainability task force and across its teams in 110 countries.

It turned out that 63% of Interface's impact on the environment was caused by the raw materials used to produce the carpet tiles – particularly nylon, an oil-based product, and tar for the backing. It made some tough decisions to let go of certain product lines and began a series of impact initiatives to eliminate waste and harmful emissions.

---

[119] Interface, 2016
[120] Hawken, 1993

A breakthrough came when Interface engaged with its supplier Aquafil, an Italian yarn manufacturer, on using recycled nylon. Together with the Zoological Society of London, it developed the 'Net-Works' programme with people from communities in the Philippines and Cameroon collecting discarded fishing nets to feed the supply chain with recycled nylon.

Production incorporating the fishing nets resulted in a 55% decrease in CO_2 for yarn, translating into a 25% reduction for the final product. The project empowers impoverished communities with additional income and long-term investment through savings in a local community bank.

After reaching its net zero mission, Interface has begun to pursue its new mission, Climate Take Back™. Since 2021, it has developed carbon-negative tiles. The 'CQuestBio' tiles backing contains carbon-negative materials made with bio-based materials and recycled fillers. The tiles enable corporate clients such as PwC in turn to reduce the carbon footprint of their offices.

Genuinely cutting emissions

Other remarkable examples lead the way to net zero. The Danish digital infrastructure provider TDC NET was the first company to receive a validated 2030 net-zero target using the Science Based Targets Initiative's Net-Zero Standard, which aligns targets with climate science.[121] TDC NET has set an ambitious target to become net-zero in its operations by 2028 and net-zero in its value chain by 2030 – two decades earlier than the ambitions set out in the Paris Agreement. Its climate roadmap focuses on energy efficiency, renewable energy, and engaging with suppliers.[122]

TDC NET takes ownership of its impact seriously. It aims to avoid additional pressure on renewable energy sources, as data volumes continue to increase. It has included 'additionality' as a mandatory requirement when procuring renewable energy. This contrasts with companies investing in Renewable Energy Credits (RECs), a specific type of Energy Attribute Certificate (EAC). These certificates prove that 1 megawatt-hour (MWh) of renewable energy has been added to the energy grid. RECs are cheaper than offsetting and allow purchasers to write off their carbon emissions without requiring them to reduce their emissions.

While purchasing RECs can help to support the renewable energy market, it tends to not actually cut emissions. To have an impact, RECs must be 'additional', meaning that the emission reductions would not have occurred without REC interventions. In reality, RECs are often not 'additional' however, because most renewable energy projects receiving revenue through RECs would be built regardless since they are already in high demand. By contrast, TDC Net's 'additionality requirement' means it will only purchase power from new renewable energy sources that are added to the grid. It signed a power purchase agreement for four new solar parks in Denmark to cover 60% of its total energy consumption in 2023.

---

[121] Sciencebasedtargets.org, 2023
[122] TDC NET case study Sciencebasedtargets.org, 2023

As a Service

Light products are notoriously designed for obsolescence. Design for obsolescence means shortening product lifespans to sell them more frequently and increase revenue.

The Phoebus Cartel is known as the first declaration between manufacturers enforcing subscriber companies to reduce the durability of lightbulbs from 2,500 hours to 1,000 hours.[123]

Design for obsolescence does not only destroy value from a customer perspective. It leads to enormous waste, emissions related to unnecessary production and unnecessary use of already scarce resources.

Several other sectors use similar design strategies for obsolescence, such as fashion, software and hardware components, smartphones, tablets, laptops, home appliances, non-refillable pens, and cars (especially recently introduced smart-connected vehicles).

Planned obsolescence was made a criminal offence in France in 2015, recognising the injustice of causing harm to our planet. However, in almost all countries worldwide, design for obsolescence is not (yet) unlawful. Thankfully, we are starting to see innovative solutions that address the intentional shortening of a product's lifespan and that are beneficial from a commercial perspective too. The Light as a Service solution by Schiphol Group in The Netherlands being a good example.

Schiphol Group aims to operate the most sustainable airports in the world, targeting zero-emissions by 2030, and energy positive airports by 2050.[124]

---

[123] Maitre-Ekern & Dalhammar, 2016; Zallio & Berry, 2017
[124] Schiphol Group, 2022

Its roadmap includes energy-positive buildings with solar power generation, phasing out gas consumption in its buildings, and operating electric buses between aircraft and terminals.[125] It further includes inspirational initiatives across their supply chain, as we will see later in this chapter. One of its initiatives illustrates how you can tackle design for obsolescence effectively.

Like most other airports, large buildings, or other organisations such as councils, Schiphol uses much light. To address the unnecessary emissions and waste related to light products being designed for a short lifespan, it reached out to its supplier Philips. It asked Philips to no longer supply light products but to provide 'Light as a Service' (LaaS) instead. This meant a contract at a fixed rate with Philips being responsible for replacing any fixtures and fittings and for paying the energy bill.

The new purchase model changed the incentive for Philips to design more durable and energy-efficient products and fixtures that are easier to replace in parts instead of the entire product. The new arrangement has reduced electricity consumption by 50% and fixtures and fittings by 75%.[126]

Kaer in Singapore uses a similar model by providing Cooling as a Service (CaaS) to companies across Asia. It reduces emissions and waste through its pay-as-you-use model and AI-driven algorithms that optimise the air-conditioning, operating only when spaces are used, saving thousands of metric tons of CO_2 annually.

The significance of this solution becomes more apparent given that the increased use of refrigeration and air conditioning plays a big part in the growth of industrial emissions – the most significant contributor to CO_2 emissions.

---

[125] Schiphol Group, 2022
[126] Philips, 2017

In addition, refrigeration and air conditioning produce hydrofluorocarbons (HFCs), potent greenhouse gases. Kaer CaaS reduces cooling energy consumption typically by 20% and in some cases up to 70%.[127]

Several other sectors have adopted the 'as a Service' model. For example, Bundles in The Netherlands leases washing machines as a service. MUD Jeans leases jeans made of organic cotton. Customers pay a 12-month lease for the trousers, after which they own them. The jeans can be returned when they are no longer wanted to either be resold or recycled.

The 'as a Service' solution can generate interesting commercial benefits such as improved customer loyalty and more predictable turnover through its subscription model. However, not all subscription models or 'as a service' models aim to tackle design for obsolescence or to reduce environmental harm. Much scope exists to improve the impact around subscription models. For example, by developing or incentivising solutions to prevent the obsolescence of laptops and computers. This could reduce the impact of carbon emissions – as well as vital environmental health hazards – significantly.

To improve the impact on our planet, can your business provide or purchase air conditioning, light, or other products using the 'as a Service' model?

Can you engage with your suppliers or customers to create awareness and amplify these types of solutions faster across our world? For example, can you make it an incentive as part of your procurement criteria?

---

[127] Ellen MacArthur Foundation, 2021

Where your laptop may end up

Some companies and organisations refurbish and donate laptops to charities as part of their sustainability strategy. At first glance, this seems a win from a social impact perspective and a win in terms of waste.

However, adopting a 'whole systems perspective' is key to creating effective impact strategies. This implies looking at not only the part that your organisation plays, but the entire end-to-end system.

Applying a whole systems perspective in this context would involve understanding how long the donated laptops are still usable by the charities to which they have been donated; as well as what happens to these laptops once they are no longer functional. The system around these products is far from circular (where waste and pollution are eliminated from the end-to-end lifecycle of a product or service).

E-waste, the waste from end-of-life electrical and electronic equipment, is a global problem that is accelerating rapidly. It is the world's fastest-growing waste stream, increasing three times faster than our population.[128] According to Global E-waste Monitor, 53.6 million metric tonnes of e-waste were generated worldwide in 2019, an increase of 17% in five years.[129] Global e-waste is estimated to reach 74.7 metric tonnes by 2030, almost double the 2014 figure, fuelled by higher electric and electronic consumption rates, shorter lifecycles, and limited repair options.

In 2019, only 17.4% of e-waste was documented officially as formally collected and recycled.[130]

---

[128] World Health Organization, 2022
[129] Global E-waste Monitor, 2020
[130] Global E-waste Monitor, 2020

Most e-waste (especially computers and laptops) is recycled informally, involving illegal exportation to countries such as China, Ghana, Nigeria, India, Thailand, the Philippines, and Vietnam. The e-waste is processed by burning specific components to recover metals such as copper.

Children are exploited in the informal e-waste sector because of their small hands to help dismantle larger quantities of e-waste, exposing them to harmful toxins.[131] Adverse health impacts on children exposed to e-waste include impaired neurodevelopment and behaviour issues, changes to respiratory, thyroid, and immune system function, DNA damage, and an increased risk of chronic illnesses when they grow up, including cancers and cardiovascular disease.[132]

Can your company engage with or incentivise your suppliers to make PCs or laptops genuinely more circular? Could your suppliers redesign these so that when they are leased 'as a Service', they are more durable, repairable, and upgradable first and foremost?

And second, can they be taken back once they are no longer useful in your business to be refurbished or remanufactured safely? Could you engage with your sector or a relevant business network to encourage manufacturers to make these improvements?

Are there other products or services that you use in your company where this model might lead to significant improvements?

---

[131] World Health Organization, 2022
[132] Parvez et al., 2021

Tackling the plastics crisis

Global plastic consumption has quadrupled over the past 30 years, with plastics production doubling since 2000 to reaching 460 million tonnes in 2019.[133] Over their lifecycle, plastics contribute 3-4% of our global greenhouse gas emissions, almost double that of the entire aviation industry.[134]

Approximately 15% of plastic waste is collected for recycling, but only 9% gets recycled; 19% is incinerated, 50% goes to landfill and 22% ends up in the environment, rivers, or seas.[135] Plastic takes more than 400 years to degrade.

Each year, about 8 million metric tonnes of plastic – about 525,600 trucks full – enter our oceans, and this rate is increasing.[136] We now have an estimated 30 million tonnes of plastic waste in our seas and oceans and 109 million tonnes accumulated in rivers. The plastics in rivers will leak into our seas for decades, even if plastic waste is significantly reduced.

Plastic is not only spoiling the beauty of our oceans and beaches. It is posing severe threats to our health and biodiversity. A million seabirds and 100,000 sea turtles, whales, and other marine mammals die every year from entanglement or digesting plastic.[137] Microplastics in seafood have entered our food chain. Scientists have only begun to scrape the surface of how the five grams of microplastics we now eat, drink, and breathe on average on a weekly basis damage our cells, guts, and overall health.

---

[133] OECD, 2022
[134] OECD, 2022, UN, 2021
[135] OECD, 2022
[136] Jambeck et al. 2013; Ellen McArthur Foundation, 2022
[137] Deloitte, 2019

So, how can we tackle the plastic crisis effectively? Initiatives like Ocean Clean-up work hard to scoop up plastic from our seas. Something that will be needed for the foreseeable future. However, it is a losing battle unless we stop the truckloads of plastic that enter our seas every minute at an increasing rate.[138] It is like the analogy of an overflowing bath. Mopping up does not make much sense unless we close the tap at the same time.

Nearly two-thirds of plastic waste comes from plastics with lifetimes of less than five years; of this 40% comes from packaging, 12% from consumer goods, and 11% from clothing and textiles.[139]

Let's look at a variety of effective innovative solutions that tackle plastic waste, carbon emissions, and other environmental issues at its root, starting with Dycle in Germany.

---

[138] Stuart, 2021
[139] OECD, 2022

True circular design

During our conversation Brieuc Saffré, CEO of design studio and consultancy lab Circulab in Paris, refers to waste as a "design mistake". He explains that, if waste is created, a critical step in the entire lifecycle of a product or service has been overlooked. When he works with business leaders some say, "…but my bottle is recyclable", Brieuc's response is: "Yes, but most bottles aren't recycled; that is the problem."

As we saw previously, only 9% of plastic gets recycled.[140]

The first principle of a circular economy is to eliminate waste and pollution.[141] The design of products and processes is critical in creating a true circular economy. It is estimated that 80% of a product's environmental impact is locked in at the design stage.[142]

Dycle in Berlin is pioneering an inspirational, fully circular solution to tackle plastic and carbon emissions related to disposable diapers (nappies). A solution that demonstrates how you can genuinely take the whole system into account.

The CO_2 and methane footprints of disposable nappies are high due to the waste and oil used for the plastic components. Each child produces around 500kg of nappy waste in their first two and half years. In Germany alone, about 12,500 trucks full of disposable nappies end up as waste each year. The estimated number of disposable nappies needed for one baby translates into approximately 1,400 litres of crude oil used for their plastic components.[143]

---

[140] https://ellenmacarthurfoundation.org/eliminate-waste-and-pollution
[141] OECD, 2022
[142] Benton and Hazell, 2013
[143] Dycle.org, 2023

Dycle has developed nappy inlays that are fully compostable. However, its 'whole systems perspective' means that it does not rely on customers composting the inlays but instead collects the used inlays in its containers. Dycle has run several trials designed around communities of about 100 families living in the same neighbourhood.

Once collected, the compostable inlays and baby poo are turned into fertile soil. With the compost, Dycle works with parents and communities to plant and fertilise fruit trees. The fruit can then be used in turn as baby food. It is a beautiful illustration of genuine circularity. Each step in the full product's lifecycle is thought through and designed to reduce emissions, prevent waste (almost) entirely, and turn this into a regenerative source.

If you rely on plastic being recycled in your products or packaging, can you develop more upstream solutions like Dycle to eliminate the use of plastic?

Or, if you are a bank, service, or investment company, can you engage with, invest in, or incentivise your suppliers or customers to implement more upstream circular solutions?

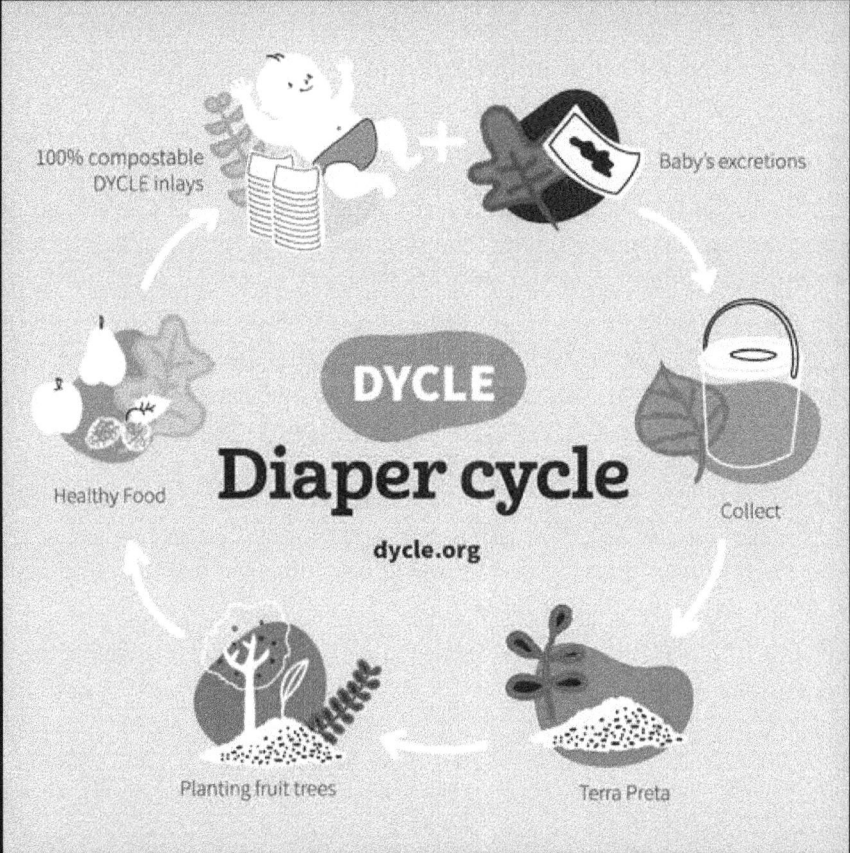

100% compostable DYCLE inlays

Baby's excretions

Healthy Food

Collect

DYCLE
Diaper cycle
dycle.org

Planting fruit trees

Terra Preta

Dycle's true circular solution, considering the whole system, Berlin, Germany

Rethinking supply chains

The Swedish Return System demonstrates superbly well what is possible by considering the broader picture and rethinking the entire supply chain.

In many sectors enormous amounts of plastic and cardboard packaging are used to distribute products across the supply chain.

To tackle this issue organisations across the grocery and retail sector in Sweden have worked together to turn the supply chain on its head. Producers no longer package products in plastic and disposable boxes for shipment to wholesalers and that are subsequently unpacked and shelved at the retailers. Instead, the Trade Association for Grocery of Sweden and the Swedish Food and Drinks Retailers Association have implemented a reusable packaging solution across the food and grocery supply chain using standardised crates, involving more than 1,500 businesses.

The new system has reduced greenhouse gas emissions by 78% compared to disposable cardboard packaging and prevents an estimated 50,000 tonnes of transport packaging waste annually.[144] The crates have a lifetime of 15 years before they are recycled.

In addition to lowering emissions, the system delivers other benefits such as reducing product damage. Moreover, stores save on average 160 working hours per year by placing the crates on the shelves directly instead of requiring staff to unpack boxes.

---

[144] Ellen MacArthur Foundation, 2021

Circular ideas & innovations

To identify circular, upstream initiatives that tackle climate change, waste, and pollution effectively in your context, you can consider the questions in the third quadrant of the IMPACT Wheel on the next page. Below, you can read about examples related to each question, ranging from quick wins to more innovative, structural solutions.

A) Reduce

The most upstream and effective way to tackle our key environmental issues is to 'reduce', first and foremost.

The reduction of waste or harmful emissions can involve solutions as simple as better conference facilities or hybrid working to reduce travel-related emissions, cycle-to-work schemes, or insulating buildings. But there are other powerful ways to reduce, such as design for durability, the 'as a Service' model, AI modelling, design for less packaging, design for using fewer materials and resources, refilling models, or by innovating the supply chain such as the Swedish Return System.

Designing products to be more durable is one of the most effective ways to cut carbon emissions related to production, packaging, storage, and transport, as well as to tackle waste and pollution. Patagonia is famous for creating high-quality, durable items that last. Even second (or third) hand Patagonia items sold on eBay hold their value. Le Creuset in France similarly produces durable pots and pans with the aim to sell 'cooking ware for a lifetime'.

We saw the 'as a Service' model as a solution to increase durability and to design for replacing parts instead of full fixtures, reducing unnecessary production and related emissions, as well as waste.

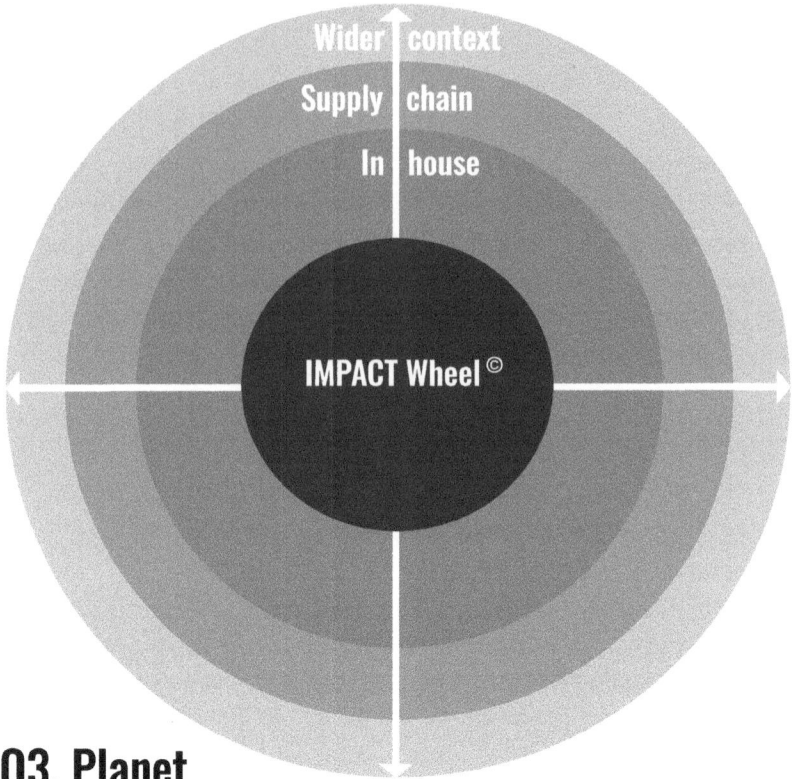

Wider context
Supply chain
In house

IMPACT Wheel ©

Q3. Planet

In house   For scarce or harmful resources and emissions, can you:

    A. Reduce? E.g.:
- Reduce travel, energy use, and water stewardship.
- Design for durability, lease models, e.g., 'as a Service'.
- AI modelling (energy, transport).
- Design for less packaging/ materials/ resources.

    B. Use better options? (E.g., renewables/ natural materials.)
    C. Re-use, redistribute, repair, refill, regenerate?
    D. Refurbish, remanufacture?
    E. Recycle, offset, RECs, carbon storage? (As a last resort.)?

Supply chain   Can you create impact by partnerships in your supply chain/ innovating supply chains?

Wider context Can you inspire, educate, invest in, or incentivise others?

AI Modelling and motion sensors are other solutions to reduce energy use, such as the example of Kaer in Singapore, for their Cooling as a Service.

TDC NET in Denmark heavily invests in more energy-efficient technologies and decommissioning legacy technology that is less efficient.

'Reducing' is also a good strategy to tackle waste, pollution, water usage, and emissions when it comes to packaging. Naked shampoo bars sold by Lush in the UK can be scanned by mobile phones for label information, eliminating the need for packaging. Lush estimates that its shampoo bars have saved 170 million plastic bottles since 2005, avoiding more than 4,000 tonnes of plastic.[145]

Bite in the US provides natural toothpaste tablets in glass pots and compostable refill bags. Everdrop in Germany has remodelled traditional cleaning products by selling cleaning tablets to be mixed with water by the consumer in reusable bottles.

Refilling stations can help to reduce packaging. At HISBE supermarket in Brighton, customers can refill products like cereals by bringing their tubs to the supermarket. Algramo in Chile uses smart-powered dispensing machines to refill household products by selling reusable bottles with chips.

Refilling models can lead to valuable commercial benefits. It tends to reduce costs for the producer, and customers often pay less. Depending on the model used, it can build brand loyalty and the producer or retailer can gather more intelligence to optimise the system and product offering.

---

[145] Lush.com, 2023

B. Use better options

'Reducing strategies' may not lead to achieving all sustainability objectives. Certain tactics, such as the leasing models, do not work well in all contexts. Interface's 'EverGreen Lease' programme is an example that allows customers to lease carpet tiles with a repair and recycling service. While the programme is still in use, it achieved more impact with its other initiatives.

Other examples are natural edible coatings that prolong the lifespan of food products like cucumber and eliminate plastic wrapping. Natural coating solutions by Apeel and Mori in the US keep moisture inside the produce and oxygen out to prolong the use by date of vegetables, meat, or fish. Ecovative in New York has developed hemp hurd and mycelium (mushroom roots) packaging to replace plastic or cardboard packaging.

C. Re-use, redistribute, regenerate

A next circular design option is to rethink systems for reuse, redistribution, or regeneration.

VYTAL in Germany provides a platform for ordering takeaways in reusable tubs. Aside from keeping the food warmer, the restaurants save between 20% and 30% in packaging costs. Customers return the reusable tubs to the restaurant at a convenient time, which increases repeat orders. VYTAL estimates that 30kg of CO_2 emissions is saved over the life cycle of one bowl, compared to single-use polystyrene or aluminium packaging.[146]

---

[146] Vytal.org, 2023

Coca-Cola in Latin America has developed a standardised reusable bottle that can be returned to retailers for a discount on their next purchase. The return rate is more than 90% and repurchase has increased by 15%. This has eliminated 1.8 billion single-use bottles in Latin America annually, reducing greenhouse gas emissions by 47% and water by 45%.[147]

D. Refurbish, remanufacture.

After finding ways to reduce, use better options and reuse, there are opportunities to refurbish or remanufacture products at the end of their lifespan. An example is Renault Re-Factory in France, dismantling around 300,000 vehicles each year. By remanufacturing parts for re-use, 80% of energy is saved compared to the production of new parts.[148]

E. Recycle, offset, RECs/EACs, carbon storage (as the last resort).

Recycling and offsetting strategies can be used as a last resort when the more upstream solutions to reduce, use better options, re-use, re-distribute, regenerate, refurbish and/or remanufacture are not possible. But it is good to be aware of potential negative implications.

Compared to more upstream solutions, recycling is the least efficient circular option, requiring energy and resources for transportation and recycling manufacturing. There are other issues, such as not all waste being separated appropriately.

---

[147] Ellen MacArthur Foundation, 2021
[148] Smart Prosperity Institute, 2021

Like recycling, offsetting carbon emissions is not an upstream solution but more like a plaster over the symptoms. It can also come with adverse side effects, with some offsetting organisations closing off lands that are territories of indigenous people, forest-dependent, peasant, and traditional communities to use these as carbon stores for net-zero claims.

As we saw earlier, Renewable Energy Credits (RECs) allow purchasers to write off their carbon emissions without requiring them to reduce their emissions. To have an impact on emission reductions however, RECs must be 'additional', meaning that the reductions in carbon emissions would not have occurred without REC interventions, which tends not to be the case. Using 'additionality' as a requirement, like TDC NET in Denmark, can help to ensure you are making an actual difference instead.

Impact your supply chains

Beyond their own operations companies can achieve significant impact by partnering with or incentivising other players in their supply chain.

Interface's partnership with Aquafil and the Zoological Society in London is a prime example. By engaging with its supplier, Interface has cut its emissions and created a wider impact, with Aquafil now selling 100% recycled nylon to other brands worldwide.

TDC NET in Denmark is making significant gains through its supplier engagement programme, with more than 3,500 suppliers worldwide. First, it assessed its suppliers and split them into two groups: high emitters and low emitters. Its initial focus is to work with the high emitters to ensure that they support TDC NET's targets and encourage them to set their targets aligned with the Science Based Target initiative before moving on to the low emitters. In addition, TDC NET hosts climate reporting workshops and regular onsite sustainability audits through the Joint Alliance for CSR, an association with 20 telecom operators worldwide.

We saw the impact of Schiphol Group collaborating with its supplier Philips on the 'Light as a Service' solution to tackle waste and emissions related to design for obsolescence. Its other supplier initiatives include working with airlines to stimulate more efficient aircrafts to reduce emissions and innovation to introduce zero-emission aircraft (battery electric, hydrogen);[149] and to encourage airlines to use sustainable aviation fuels with differentiated charges, rewarding quieter, cleaner aircrafts. At Schiphol Airport, aircrafts with an inferior environmental performance pay airport charges that are up to five times higher.[150]

---

[149] Schiphol Group, 2022
[150] Schiphol Group, 2022

Impact in wider contexts

Inspiring or educating others.

Finally, you could consider impact initiatives that inspire or educate parties beyond your supply chain. This works particularly well for companies that lead on sustainability in their sector. Interface established the 'Rays' initiative which allows companies to visit Interface and learn from its stories and experiences. Following their success in reducing emissions, Interface Founder Ray Anderson served as co-chair of the President's Council on Sustainable Development during President Clinton's administration, and the Presidential Climate Action Plan during President Obama's administration. Interface further widened its impact as part of UN Partnerships and EU lobbying.

Beyond its supplier engagements, TDC NET was among the founders of the European Green Digital Coalition, a consortium of ICT companies seeking to support green and digital transformation. The coalition is committed to investing in developing green digital solutions with a net positive impact, by developing methods and tools to measure the impact of green technologies and co-creating guidelines for the green digital transformation of other sectors.

Schiphol Group is active in several partnerships to advocate for more progressive mandates for Sustainable Aviation Fuel in Europe, and to support research and investment of cleaner aviation. An example of this is advancing the development of synthetic kerosene through direct air capture. The Group's sustainability roadmap further includes opening an experience centre at Schiphol Airport to educate passengers about sustainable aviation and offer opportunities to purchase Sustainable Aviation Fuel for their flights.

Investing in or incentivise good practices.

Online portals or service providers, such as investment firms, banks, accountants, and consulting firms, have an opportunity to help resolve our global challenges by encouraging customers, suppliers, and other relevant parties to implement effective solutions as outlined in the previous three chapters, as well as the next one.

Imagine the impact Amazon could have by charging lower distribution fees on its platform to suppliers that impact our world more positively than others. The effectiveness of such incentives would depend on the criteria used, and whether they take key success factors into account.

NatWest Bank provides sustainable finance options including green loans for companies at attractive rates to invest in clean energy solutions. Incentive criteria could be aimed at reducing carbon emissions, design for durability versus obsolescence, or eliminating harmful materials or emissions. To help address other global challenges incentives could extend to impactful practices in the other three quadrants of the IMPACT Wheel including empowerment, just payments, and health and wellbeing. An example is Triodos Bank encouraging more just CEO-to-average-worker pay gaps across the companies in which it invests.

Investment companies have an opportunity to grow their financial return as well as their positive impact on the world by playing into the fast-growing impact investment market. This market segment has grown more than tenfold in the past five years, estimated at $1.164 trillion USD in 2022. While still relatively small it is the fastest growing category in the financial space.[151] The steep growth is expected to continue with demand driven especially among younger generations who seek to align financial resources with their personal interests and values.

---

[151] Impact Investing Institute, 2022

"

If you leave a pot of capital behind in a world where there's no fresh water and the oceans are collapsing and there is no air to breathe and we have social unrest because of the income disparity, it's not the legacy that your grandchildren are going to be able to use.

So helping in the creation of a better world is a far better legacy than leaving behind a big pot of money.

Margaret McGovern, former CEO PYMWYMIC,
European Impact Investment Fund

As this rapidly developing market segment grows and matures it will become even more important for impact investors as well as investees to ensure that they tackle global issues effectively and to measure their impact returns and financial returns.

Chintan Panchal, Co-Founder of RCPK, a law firm that offers guidance to impact-driven investors and businesses explains: "Synthesizing multiple bottom lines requires an even greater degree of rigor compared to traditional investing. An investor who is deeply informed about the financial and impact prospects of an investment opportunity, as well as how those objectives interact with each other when the enterprise is stressed, and who is able to build thoughtful accountability into their transactions will stand a better chance of successfully monetizing their investments in the long run."[152]

Impact investment can at times take longer to pay off. During our interview Margaret McGovern, at the time CEO of a European Impact Investment Fund called PYMWYMIC, refers to impact investment as "patient capital".

She explains: "Largely impact businesses take longer than normal venture capital. So long term outlook is a really good thing to have. You need to have patience, basically, with these companies."

---

[152] Forbes, 2017

While it can take longer for impact investments to create a return, that does not mean that these investments are less lucrative than traditional investments. As we saw in the Unilever versus Kraft Heinz case, as well as the comparison between Costco and Walmart, companies with more positive impact can create a significantly better return, particularly when measured over the longer term. Investment portfolios that incorporate companies with higher ESG scores also proof to be more resilient.[153]

In Chintan Panchal's words: "A misconception is the idea that impact investing means concessionary or below market investing. It can be, but the majority of investors in the space seek and achieve returns that outperform their traditional benchmarks."[154]

---

[153] BofAML, 2019
[154] Forbes, 2017

In a nutshell

1. To combat climate change, there is much scope to make improvements in 'industry' and 'buildings', the largest contributing sectors of global greenhouse gas emissions at 24.2% and 17.5% respectively.[155] Industrial processes are the fastest growing source of greenhouse gas emissions at 203% growth since 1990, and electricity and heating are the second fastest growing source at 84% growth since 1990.[156]

2. Inspirational examples around the globe lead the way in achieving 'net zero' such as TDC Net, or even in going beyond 'net zero', such as Interface.

3. Besides climate change, companies impact our planet severely in terms of air pollution, the plastics crisis, loss of biodiversity, water pollution and scarcity, and increased scarcity of other resources.

4. To tackle environmental issues effectively requires 'whole systems thinking' and upstream circular design solutions. The questions in the third quadrant of the IMPACT Wheel on page 108, and the examples throughout this chapter can be used to trigger ideas for effective impact initiatives. Initiatives that tackle the root cause of our key environmental issues, as opposed to dealing with symptoms, to create more structural, lasting outcomes and a better impact return.

---

[155] OurWorldInData, 2023.
[156] Climate Watch, 2023; The World Resources Institute, 2023.

Chapter Five

Health and wellbeing

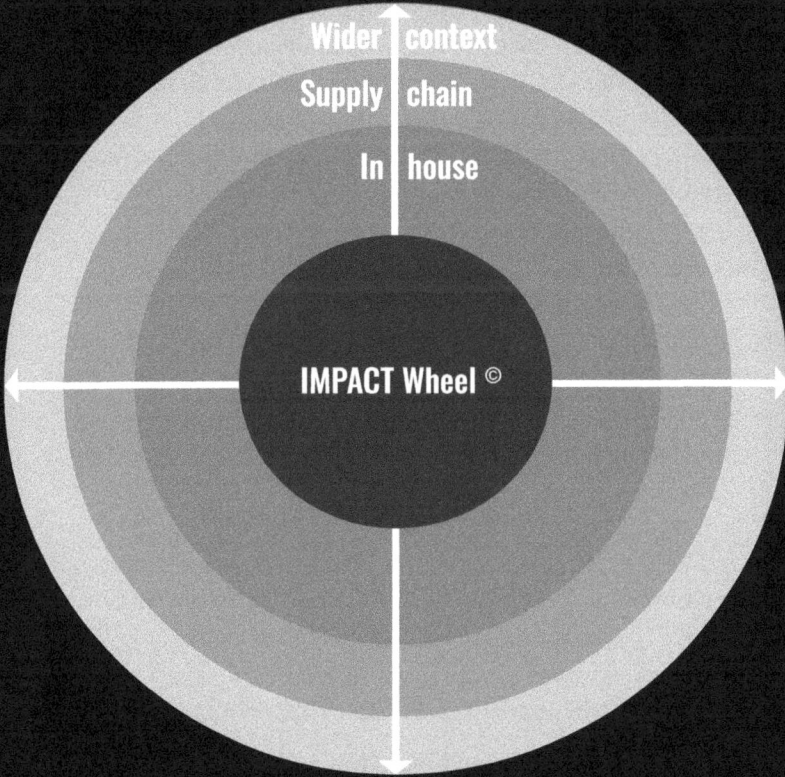

Wider context
Supply chain
In house

IMPACT Wheel ©

Q4. Health and Wellbeing

The four quadrants of the IMPACT Wheel relate to each other. In particular, initiatives in the first three quadrants in the IMPACT Wheel tend to have strong knock-on effects on the fourth quadrant, 'health and wellbeing'.

Empowerment, the first quadrant, impacts health and wellbeing. When parents from impoverished communities are empowered with economic opportunities, this impacts their families' physical and mental health. The economic opportunities created by Grassroutes or SoleRebels not only address the first UN SDG, 'No Poverty'; they also create positive knock-on effects on related SDGs such as 'Zero hunger' and 'Health and wellbeing', for example, by being in a better position to pay for food and medical care. Empowerment opportunities at Brigade, Ctalents, and Goodwill Solutions, improve the quality of life of the apprentices and employees as well as their family members.

Similarly, Just Payments – the second quadrant – impacts health and wellbeing. And not only in terms of people on the unfortunate end of rising inequality. Selfish practices that we have been conditioned to in much of how we do business do not do justice to the essence of human beings. Scientific studies show that people who work in a context where they are 'selfish beyond fairness' damage their own mental and physical wellbeing and shorten their life expectancy.[157] Research reveals that people in companies with fairer practices have a higher life expectancy and fewer incidences of cardiovascular disease.[158] Interestingly, retirees at employee-owned companies such as John Lewis and Mondragón are found to live longer than retirees from non-employee-owned companies.[159]

The third quadrant, the impact of a business on our planet, has significant consequences on health and wellbeing. First, 99% of our global population is exposed to air pollution exceeding the safe guideline level.[160] According to the World Health Organisation, an estimated 4.2 million deaths globally are linked to ambient (outdoor) air pollution, mainly from heart disease,

---

[157] Crocker et al., 2017
[158] Erdal, 2014
[159] Erdal, 2014
[160] World Health Organisation, 2023b

stroke, chronic obstructive pulmonary disease (COPD), lung cancer, and acute respiratory infections. Air pollution is estimated to be responsible for 19% of global cardiovascular deaths, 21% of deaths due to stroke, 24% of deaths from coronary heart disease, 43% of COPD cases and deaths worldwide, and 29% of all lung cancer cases and deaths.[161]

Climate change is expected to cause 250,000 annual deaths due to heat stress, particularly amongst people with cardiovascular or respiratory conditions.[162] An estimated 60,000 annual deaths are expected due to extreme weather that has tripled since 1960.[163]

Our guts, cells, and health are impacted by the estimated 5 grams of microplastics we breathe, eat, and drink on average weekly.[164] Aside from that, some plastic components emit harmful toxins from their manufacture to their disposal. For example, the production of PVC creates dioxin – a highly toxic pollutant – and dioxin-like compounds. Dioxin also gets released during bleaching processes of materials such as cotton.

Dioxins are found throughout the world. These toxic compounds can cause cancer, reproductive and developmental problems, damage the immune system, and interfere with hormones.[165] Dioxin accumulates in the fatty tissue of animals exposed to the polluted atmosphere. The toxins do not only impact biodiversity loss this way but also enter the food chain. More than 90% of human exposure is through food, mainly by eating meat and dairy products, fish, and shellfish.

Aside from impact initiatives in the first three quadrants of the IMPACT Wheel, companies can use the fourth quadrant of the IMPACT Wheel to identify ways to improve the health and wellbeing of people as part of their teams, across their supply chains, and a wider context.

---

[161] World Health Organisation, 2023b
[162] WHO, 2018
[163] WHO, 2018
[164] WWF, 2022; Ellen MacArthur Foundation, 2016
[165] EPA, 2023; World Health Organization, 2016

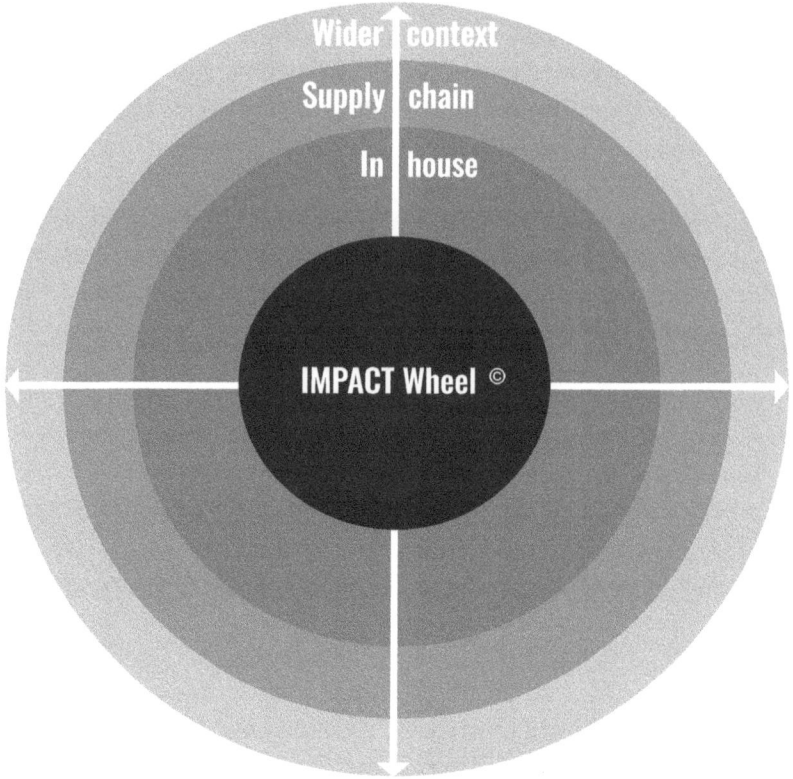

Wider context

Supply chain

In house

IMPACT Wheel ©

Q4. Health & wellbeing

In house   Can you create more positive impact through:

- Working conditions, health & wellbeing policies.
- Healthy food options,
- Facilities (light, air quality, interior design, furniture),
- Products/ packaging/ materials/ ingredients,
- Production methods?

Supply chain   Can you create impact by procuring from suppliers with better impact on health & wellbeing/ incentivise suppliers?

Wider context   Can you inspire, educate, incentivise, or invest in others?

Health and wellbeing in house

SAP, a global software and technology based in Germany, has won employee awards worldwide, scooping up 154 awards in 2022 alone.[166] Health and wellbeing is a key pillar of SAP's business strategy. Employee wellbeing is a top objective for the CEO, Board of Directors, and front-line managers. SAP explains that the mission of its staff wellbeing strategy is "to enable sustainable business success by shaping a caring, healthy, and inclusive culture".

SAP measures the impact of its wellbeing efforts by its Business Health Culture Index, which climbed from 69% in 2013 to 81% in 2022. Each percentage change in the index has delivered an impact on its operating profit of between €90 million and €100 million Euros.[167] The index covers questions concerning how employees rate their personal wellbeing and the working conditions at SAP, including leadership culture.

Key health management focus areas at SAP are stress management, self-management, work-life balance support, personal resilience, a psychologically safe work environment, an ergonomically safe office set up, travel medicine, pandemic management, vaccinations, road safety, and general medical prevention for all generations.

Examples of health and wellbeing initiatives are paid family leave, a return-to-work-programme, on-site childcare facilities, parent coaching, flexible work hours, a dinner to-go programme where staff can order healthy meals to take home, mental health programme, mindfulness workshops, and emotional intelligence workshops.

---

[166] SAP Integrated Report, 2022
[167] Forbes, 2019; SAP, 2022

Aside from Patagonia's world-leading efforts to fulfil its mission to "save our planet", it is well known for excellent working conditions, including good salaries, work-life balance' practices such as on-site childcare, surfing, yoga, and subsidies to purchase hybrid vehicles. In return, Patagonia receives about 9,000 resumes for each vacancy without advertising it, avoiding recruitment costs, and creating a competitive advantage by attracting talented staff.

Similarly, Ikea's flexible work schedules, job sharing, and compressed working weeks are credited with increased productivity and lower recruitment and marketing costs due to motivated staff, leading to high standards in customer service.[168] Typically, companies that invest more than their peers in staff and that create more value for people and planet incur lower costs related to marketing, recruitment, and staff turnover.[169]

Aside from working conditions and work-life balance policies and practices, companies impact the health and wellbeing of their teams by the design and management of their workspaces. Employees spend many hours at work, so the design of a workspace can impact the health and wellbeing of teams significantly and, in turn, their productivity.

Spacebloom, a design company based in Brussels, supports businesses to improve their layout and interior design to create positive impact on the health and wellbeing of their teams, as well as the environment. Its sustainable design framework[170] includes criteria for air quality, thermal comfort, light, ergonomics, active furniture, design for mental health, access to nature, art, restorative design, hydration and nutrition, accessibility, and safety. Apart from the impact of a workspace on the health and wellbeing of its occupants Spacebloom's framework includes criteria such as energy efficiency, adaptive reuse and sustainable sourcing, water and waste management, to benefit the health of our planet.

---

[168] Sisodia et al., 2014
[169] Sisodia et al., 2014
[170] https://www.spacebloom.co/

Supply chain

Beyond the wellbeing of their teams, companies have opportunities to improve the health and wellbeing of people across their supply chains.

For a start, ingredients, materials, and production processes can impact our health significantly. In many cases the harmful options are cheaper. An example is traditional cotton, which is produced by using toxic chemicals. A substantial 10% of all agricultural chemicals in the US are used for cotton production.[171] Organic cotton is more costly but less harmful to our planet and the workers on the cotton farms. Companies committed to creating more positive impact, such as Patagonia and Mud Jeans, use organic cotton instead of cheaper but harmful traditional cotton. HISBE supermarket only stocks products that do not harm its customers' health.

Can your business improve health and wellbeing by altering your procurement, ingredients, materials, processes, or policies?

Can you incentivise suppliers to improve their impact on health and wellbeing as part of your procurement criteria?

As a supermarket, a distribution platform, a bank, a management consultancy, or an insurance company, could you offer better rates to those that positively impact health and wellbeing?

---

[171] Sisodia et al., 2014

Wider context

Companies can create an impact in a wider context by encouraging responsible consumption, particularly for addictive products that can be harmful. The docudrama *A Social Dilemma* tells the story of how some social media companies create targeted algorithms to make people's online experience as addictive as possible, building on the dopamine hits they get from 'likes' and reactions as social validation.

The docudrama explains how the more hooked social media users become to spend time online, the more money can be made through data mining, advertising, and selling our data. Such data shows, for example, how people can be influenced to buy things or how to be persuaded to vote a certain way.

Some risks involved with extensive social media use are increased polarisation of societies, as we are fed information that fits our beliefs.[172] There is also evidence of a correlation (but not necessarily a proven causation) between social media use and mental health issues and suicide rates, with users becoming too focused on external validation. This is evident particularly among children and adolescents.[173]

Can your business campaign, encourage, or educate people to improve health and wellbeing?

Can you inspire, incentivise, or invest in others to improve their impact on health and wellbeing?

---

[172] Grover, 2022; Jung & Sangwon, 2023; Kubin & von Sikorski, 2021
[173] Cunningham et al., 2021; McCrae et al., 2017; Marino et al., 2018; Swedo et al., 2021

In a nutshell

1. The four quadrants of the IMPACT Wheel relate to each other. Particularly the impact of a business on our planet impacts our health and wellbeing. Examples include increased mortality and illness due to climate change, air pollution, microplastics, or toxins such as dioxin entering our food chain.

2. Organisations can significantly impact the health and wellbeing of the people in their teams. The example of SAP shows how investing in the health and wellbeing of staff can lead to substantial higher profitability.

3. Beyond in house initiatives, companies can impact health and wellbeing across their supply chains, by opting to purchase products or materials from suppliers that are not harmful to people's health, such as organic cotton instead of traditional cotton. Alternatively, businesses can choose to work with sustainable suppliers, or partner with suppliers to create more positive impact.

4. Business leaders can impact health and wellbeing significantly in a wider context by educating or encouraging people to consume responsibly, or by incentivising or investing in other organisations to create more of a positive impact.

Chapter Six

Leading like a genius

Illustration by Silvan Borer

Our planet Earth is 4.5 billion years old. If we scale this back to 45 years, humanity has only been here for less than a day, and our Industrial Revolution started just one minute ago.

We have achieved some impressive things on our planet in 'less than a day'. We can predict the weather reasonably accurately. Basic needs such as warmth and food could be met for all. We have developed advanced technology to support medical care. There are many ways to travel, visit wonderful places and meet people from various cultures. And we can enjoy vast amounts of high-quality entertainment and comfort.

We have also caused much harm – particularly in the past 'one minute' since the Industrial Revolution. Such as increased social unrest, crime rates, and polarisation of our societies due to the rising income disparity. Such as air pollution, plastic pollution, the release of harmful chemical toxins, humanitarian crises caused by climate impacts, droughts, rising sea levels, flooding, and extreme heat. And such as a massive loss of biodiversity, risking the collapse of entire ecosystems. Some of the consequences are already irreversible. Once a species is extinct, there is no way to bring it back.

Looking at where we are from a big-picture perspective, we can see the importance of how we will manage to evolve our economic system during the next 'one minute' on our planet.

If we drill down to the essence, a major flaw in our current system is exposed. This flaw stems from a mistake that we have made in implementing our free market economies; a crucial error about which Adam Smith, father of our free market system, in fact, warned us…

Adam Smith's warning

In more recent years, awareness has increased about some of the negative consequences of the Industrial Revolution – such as climate change, pollution and rising inequality. Adam Smith has been accused by some of being the culprit, implying that his suggestion to pursue 'self-interest' as the engine of a free-market system has become a justification for a harmful economic system that is based on greed.[174]

By studying Smith's books, it becomes evident that he did not imply an economic system where self-interest is a justification to ignore harm to societies and our planet. In fact, by reading his 'Theory of Moral Sentiments' it becomes clear that we have made the crucial error he warned us not to make in implementing a free market economy.[175]

Let me explain.

Smith suggested a free-market system in which the drive towards profit efficiently allocates resources around market demand. Simply put, he suggested that it is more efficient for a baker to produce the bread and cakes aligned with customer's demand, with profits as an incentive, than for a centralised institution to decide what the baker must produce.

Smith argued that self-interest in this context has merit, in that the drive for profits encourages business to create better products and services. He reasoned that the drive for profits incentivises our efforts and resources into innovating and aligning supply efficiently around our needs.

---

[174] Klein, 2015; Macey, J, 2014; Malm, 2015; Monbiot, 2017; Moore, 2015; Rothschild, E. 2023; Verburg, 2018
[175] Smith, 1759: 84

Smith did not suggest however that 'self-interest' is a justification to pursue profits by abusing power to exploit employees or parties involved across supply chains. Nor did he suggest that companies should be free to harm our planet or people's health to maximise profits.

On the contrary, Smith emphasised that free market economies can only function with strong principles of justice.

He said: "Justice is the main pillar that upholds the whole edifice. If it is removed, the great, the immense fabric of human society, that fabric which to raise and support seems in this world, to have been the peculiar and darling care of Nature, must in a moment crumble into atoms."[176]

It is those 'justice principles', emphasised by Smith, which are largely missing in our free market economies. And what has caused much of the havoc in our world. Incorporating justice principles fully is also the key to resolving many of the critical global issues we face today.

---

[176] Smith, 1759: 84

"

Free market economies can only function with strong principles of justice. Otherwise, our societies must crumble into atoms.[177]

Adam Smith

The four pillars of justice

The IMPACT Wheel comprises the four key areas where businesses can tackle the root cause of our key global issues effectively. The types of initiatives and practices that help to 'close the tap' of our UN SDGs instead of dealing with the symptoms. Looking more closely at the four quadrants in the IMPACT Wheel, we see that each is founded on justice.

First, justice demands to offer 'equal opportunities' by empowering people and communities to contribute their skills and potential to society. Adam Smith talked in 1776 already about enabling people to use their potential as "the most sacred property".

He said: "The property which every man has in his own labour, as it is the original foundation of all other property, so it is the most sacred and inviolable. To hinder a poor man from employing his strength and dexterity in what manner he thinks proper, without injury to his neighbour, is a plain violation of the most sacred property."[178]

Second, justice implies that jointly created wealth is distributed *fairly* between the key players involved by paying people 'their dues'. According to the principle of equity, a fair economic system distributes payments in proportion to a party's contribution, as opposed to the level of power.[179] This concerns wealth creation within an organisation as well as a supply chain. Essentially, the question behind deciding how much we pay suppliers, or what we charge customers, or salary levels should be 'what is fair and just based on the contribution made by each party?', instead of 'what can we get away with?'.

This may sound controversial. Negotiating supplier prices, fees or salaries based on a position of power, has become largely the norm and tends to be celebrated – even if it perpetuates or causes poverty, child labour or

---

[178] Smith, 1776: 127
[179] Maiese, 2020

rising inequality. But just because something is the norm does not mean it is right. Calls to stop slavery, apartheid, and women getting the right to vote were controversial not that long ago too, but we evolved by realising how unjust these were.

Third, justice demands not to harm human rights or our planet. In 1987, the Brundtland Commission defined this as "meeting the needs of the present generation without compromising the ability of future generations to meet their own needs".[180]

New laws are being implemented, such as France's legislation making design for obsolescence a criminal offence; tax penalties in some US States and Israel for large CEO-average-worker-pay-gaps; or the participation law in The Netherlands to support social inclusion. But mostly there remains a lack of legislation around the core justice principles.

The lack of justice in our free-market economies has fed the rising inequality and all its implications on social unrest, crime rates, and polarisation of our societies. It contributes to poverty and child labour. It has caused biodiversity loss, pollution, the climate crisis, displacement of people and millions of deaths each year consequently.

Had we implemented Smith's philosophy, companies would compete to create superior products and services. They would compete on efficient and effective management. But we would not allow injustice to be part of the norm in how we trade and do business. We would not be paying farmers or creators too little for what they contribute to the supply chain, nor would we use a powerful position to overcharge customers, or cause harm to people and planet by using certain materials or processes.

The way to resolve many of our key global issues structurally and prevent others, is to rebalance our free market economies with firm principles of justice: the way Adam Smith suggested in the first place.

---

[180] Brundtland Commission, 1987

Creating the best return

Balancing profits with justice principles is not only the key to rebalancing our free-market economies and resolving our global issues; it is also the key to creating a better long-term return on investment.

The examples of Unilever versus Kraft Heinz and Costco versus Walmart we saw earlier illustrate how a more positive impact on people and the planet leads to a significantly better return on investment.[181] Increasing numbers of studies demonstrate the business case of companies investing in creating a more positive impact.[182]

The same applies the other way around. We saw how initiatives with an impact mission achieve better outcomes when they pursue their purpose as well as profits 'as part of a whole'. In Chapter Two, we saw that companies like Ctalents, Goodwill Solutions, and Brigade and Beyond Food show a more robust financial platform as well as 300% to 400% higher success rates in terms of their impact compared to those with a similar mission and context, but that lack a sound commercial model. Initiatives that show the best outcomes each strike an excellent balance in integrating both 'profits and purpose'.

It is exactly like the common trait that Albert Rothenberg discovered in what sets geniuses like Einstein, Picasso, van Gogh, Edison, Da Vinci and Mozart apart from their peers: "The pursuit of the unity of opposites."[183]

The ancient yin-yang concept symbolises the virtue of balancing opposites, demonstrating a synergistic relationship.[184]

---

[181] Forbes, 2020; Polman & Winston, 2021; Unilever, 2018
[182] BlackRock, 2019; Deloitte, 2019; Kantar, 2020, Morgan Stanley, 2018; Sisodia, Wolfe, and Sheth, 2014; Whelan & Kronthal-Sacco, 2019
[183] Rothenberg, 1979
[184] Lewis, 2000, Schad et al., 2016

If we consider how our brains work, we realise why it is still so rare for business leaders to get this balance right. When confronted with what we perceive as opposites, the human brain is wired to see either one or the other predominantly.

We tend to perceive either a business that maximises profits but with a separate goal to 'give back' through CSR or sustainability initiatives; or an 'impact business' or 'social enterprise' that does something good but with a commercial model as a secondary vehicle. But those with the best outcomes *pursue both equally, integrated throughout the business model*.

To balance profit maximisation and a purpose effectively as part of a whole to achieve the best outcomes for people and the planet, we can identify guidelines that differentiate 'GOOD vs. BAD profits'.

GOOD vs. BAD profits

It is easy to be drawn into pursuing profits without sufficient emphasis on purpose, given that our brains are hardwired to see one or the other when faced with opposites.

Our education and conditioning mean it is not straightforward for us to make decisions that involve a trade-off between profits and value for society and planet. Equally, from the other angle, recognising and incorporating sound profit drivers can be challenging for 'impact initiatives' or 'sustainability initiatives' to achieve a more robust financial platform and better impact outcomes.

If we look at different ways to maximise profits, we can differentiate drivers that meet the nature of justice, from others that do not. The following guidelines can be applied to balancing profits and a business's impact on our world. They are general rules of thumb for 'leading like a genius'.

Profit maximisation, in its simplest form, implies maximising revenue and minimising costs. Let's assess which different ways to increase revenue and to reduce costs meet justice principles and which do not. BAD profit drivers are practices towards maximising profits that do not meet core justice principles. These include:

Battle for unjust payments, pricing and salary levels based on power.

Afflict harm by using harmful ingredients, resources, or processes.

Design for obsolescence, addiction, or irresponsible consumption.

On the other hand, 'leading like a genius' requires GOOD profit drivers. Those that are not unjust. These are important to incorporate as part of your business model and initiatives to achieve successful outcomes, regardless of a social or environmental purpose. These include:

Get rid of *unnecessary* costs.

Offer products/ services aligned with market demand.

Operate efficiently and effectively.

Drive impact throughout but position it as the 'cherry on the cake'.

It is unlikely that Ctalents would have been as successful if it focused less on aligning its candidates' talents with its clients' vacancy requirements. It is unlikely that Brigade and Beyond Food would have been as successful if it did not balance the number of apprentices with experienced chefs.

It is unlikely that Goodwill Solutions would have been listed in the FTSE fastest growing companies in Europe and achieved outstanding success rates in transforming people's lives if its clients did not value its logistics services. Tony's Chocolonely would have been less likely to have grown as fast if its chocolate flavours were not as tasty or well marketed. Interface would unlikely be market leader if the quality of their modular flooring was not valued as much, regardless of its environmental mission.

Finally, companies with the best outcomes regarding profits and purpose position their impact as the 'cherry on the cake'. While they drive impact as an integrated part of their business model, it is not the primary purchase motivation of their customers. Customers eat at Brigade because they love the food and ambiance. Goodwill Solutions' clients such as Amazon and M&S buy its logistics services because of its excellent quality.

Value for people or planet can however undoubtedly play an essential role in increasing revenue by boosting customer loyalty and referral rates. As Sandra Ballij, Founder and CEO of Ctalents says: "It is not the reason why customers come, but it is the reason why they become a fan."

In a nutshell

1. Since the Industrial Revolution, business has contributed to climate change, pollution, rising inequality, the perpetuation of poverty, and severe impacts on our health and wellbeing.

2. Much harm could have been avoided had we listened to Adam Smith's warning that "free market economies can only function with strong principles of justice". Humanity will face huge threats unless we rebalance our system by incorporating core principles of justice. The IMPACT Wheel's quadrants are each founded on pillars of justice.

3. Pursuing profits and justice 'as part of a whole' is not only a structural way to effectively resolve many of our key global issues. It is also the key to achieving a better return on investment longer term. Companies with the best outcomes 'lead like a genius' by pursuing profits and purpose as an integrated part of their business model.

4. We can differentiate 'GOOD vs. BAD profits' to integrate profits with justice. BAD profit drivers do not meet justice principles:

    Battle for unjust payments, pricing and salary levels based on power.

    Afflict harm by using harmful ingredients, resources, or processes.

    Design for obsolescence, addiction, or irresponsible consumption.

GOOD profit drivers, on the other hand, are not unjust and are essential to achieve successful outcomes. These include:

Get rid of *unnecessary* costs.

Offer products/ services aligned with market demand.

Operate efficiently and effectively.

Drive impact throughout but position it as the 'cherry on the cake'.

Chapter Seven

IMPACT roadmap

"

Real change, enduring change, happens one step at a time.

Ruth Bader Ginsburg,

Former Associate Justice of the Supreme Court of the US

5 steps to IMPACT success

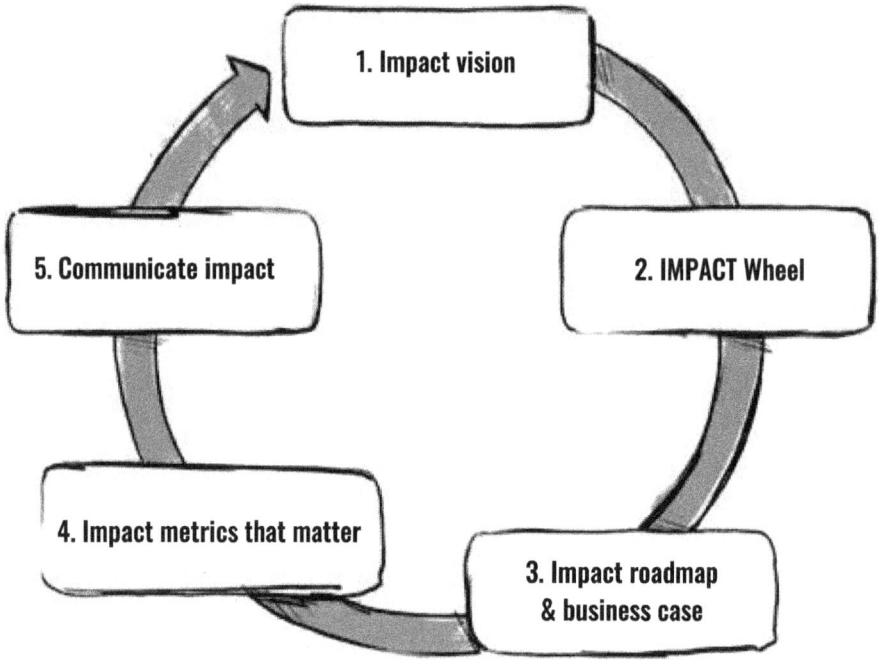

A seagoing compass has a gimble levelling device that keeps it steady at sea, particularly when the ship hits rough waters. A good compass is invaluable for a captain to keep a boat on course.

This final chapter provides a five-step framework that can be used to develop a clear compass for your impact journey. It offers practical tools to refine your impact vision, develop an effective impact roadmap and business case, identify impact metrics that matter, and develop an authentic communications plan to boost business growth.

Photography by davidboni.com.

Impact vision

When reflecting on Interface's sustainability journey, its former Founder and Chairman Ray Anderson credits its success partly to its bold vision. He explains: "When you hold up a vision that is so outrageous that it takes the breath away. When people are gasping, 'What did he just say?'. It has taken us to places that we would have never dreamt of." He explains how his company's ambitious vision unleashed creativity and energy throughout the whole organisation.

Setting out on an impact journey without defining a vision is like a ship setting sail without coordinates for the direction of the journey. First, a vision enables you to communicate the direction of your set course. If you can align your vision with the intrinsic motivation of the people in your business, it will enable you to tap into an engine that is hugely powerful. Second, a clear vision is essential in prioritising initiatives and preventing getting bogged down into projects that do not achieve essential outcomes. Third, it will help as a navigation point throughout your sustainability journey, particularly when you hit rougher waters.

Liam Black has oodles of experience dealing with the challenges in balancing profits and purpose as previous CEO of Jamie Oliver's Fifteen and several other ventures, and as mentor to many entrepreneurs and business leaders who aim to make a positive impact. As we discuss the key factors to overcome these challenges he stresses: "If you don't know what your purpose is and you haven't really articulated it, and then you have a crisis, which all businesses do, how do you get back? You have nothing to get back to. So, articulate what your purpose is very carefully, make sure everyone understands it. You cannot communicate it enough."

Your vision is the finish line, the end game, the ultimate impact you want to create for our world. Patagonia's core purpose is 'we're in business to save our home planet'. Aravind Eye Care's vision is 'to eliminate needless blindness'. Tony's Chocolonely aims to 'eliminate all illegal labour, including child labour, in the cocoa supply chain'.

"

SHOOT FOR THE MOON

The more ambitious and aspirational your mission, the greater its power. Be unreasonable. Don't settle for incremental goals. If you want to transform something, set a goal you don't know how to achieve yet.

Moonshot goals can be uncomfortable. But moonshot goals can also be transformational for your people and your business.

We dared to imagine a business with no negative environmental impact. It was an ambition people could rally around. It created passion and the innovative thinking needed to get there. And it gave us a clear vision and definition of success. The results speak for themselves.

Ray Anderson, Founder, Interface

The impact vision can be the intrinsic purpose of a Founder. Or, to refine your vision, consider running a workshop with your management team, or all teams, preferably offsite. In my experience, offsite workshops work better than meeting in the workplace, as it allows people the time and space to focus on the bigger picture. Some companies prefer engaging all staff in these workshops to build on everyone's creativity and experience and develop buy-in from the whole team. Others prefer working with 'champions' who represent various teams. The right approach depends on a business's stage, size, and culture. You may want to use external facilitators to help guide you through this process or manage it in house.

One way to brainstorm your impact vision is to ask the 'five whys'.[185] This technique was originally developed by Sakichi Toyoda, Founder of Toyota, who stated that "by repeating why five times, the nature of the problem as well as its solution becomes clear."[186] This is like unpeeling the layers of an onion to get to its core. You can start with a descriptive statement of what impact you aim to achieve and then ask, 'Why?' several times.

For example, Patagonia makes durable clothing. Why is that important? Well, making durable clothing prevents waste. Why is it important to prevent waste? And so on.

After a few whys (not necessarily five whys), you'll find you're getting down to the organisation's fundamental purpose. In Patagonia's case: 'we are in business to save our home planet'. You might get to the core in five whys, but it might take three, four, or six or seven whys. Review all the different answers with your team, searching for what resonates most, what generates passion, and what gets to the heart of your purpose.

Neuro-linguistic programming (NLP) techniques such as relaxation and visualisation can help to access your intrinsic motivation and the creative and unrestricted part of the brain.

---

[185] Collins & Porras, 1996; Taiichi, 2006
[186] Taiichi, 2006

"

If you imagine it,
some day it will happen.
If you don't imagine it,
it will never happen.

Professor Muhammad Yunus, Nobel Peace Prize Laureate,
Founder Grameen Bank, Bangladesh

A primary role of core ideology is to guide and inspire. It helps to guide your decision-making and attract and motivate the employees who fit well within your company culture.

Patagonia's vision guides its strategy, products, processes, and culture. Being in business 'to save our home planet' translates not just into durable clothing but also into leading the way in using renewable energy in all facilities, using organic cotton as opposed to traditional cotton, and campaigns to raise awareness about environmental issues. It is about being clear who you are as a company and what you stand for, regardless of any changes in the world.

Guiding questions to uncover or refine your impact vision could be:

1.   What problem would you like to solve if you had unlimited money?

2.   When you're 90 and look back, what would you feel immensely proud of? What would you regret not having contributed to?

3.   Particularly thinking of your grandchildren, and those of others, is there anything you would regret not helping to address?

4.   Imagine your company winning a prize for your impact; what kind of legacy springs to mind that you have created?

5.   Are there any global or local issues to which you feel drawn?

6.   How can you as a person and your particular strengths and talents be of benefit to the wider world?

7.   What strengths can your business use to benefit the key global and local issues we face?

8.   If you had a 25-year time frame, what could your organisation do to maximise its positive impact on society and the environment?

As part of gathering my data, I met Eduardo Balarezo in the beautiful Galapagos Islands. Eduardo founded his business Lonesome George & Co to support conservation of the stunning UNESCO Heritage site. In their office on the main island Eduardo and his team shared many valuable insights based on their journey. One of Eduardo's lines has stuck with me, even without revisiting it during the later transcription and analysis stages: "Sustainability is not a destination. Sustainability is a trajectory. You can never say "I made it", because you can always improve."

It is worth considering where your business is positioned and wants to be on the sustainability spectrum, as visualised on the next page. With on the one end harm and destruction caused by rising pay gaps and widening inequality, depleting resources, the growing plastic pollution crisis, toxic emissions, or climate change; and on the other end proactively tackling our global issues by empowering people into jobs, by leading on Just Payments, innovating or scaling up green and regenerative solutions, or by improving health and wellbeing.

Another worthwhile consideration is at what stage in the adoption curve you want to tackle certain global issues. Everett Rogers identified five stages for adopting new innovations: Innovators, Early Adopters, Early Majority, Late Majority, and Laggards. Stronger competitive advantages are gained by taking an 'early adopter' versus 'late adopter' role. Staff, customers, investors, and other stakeholders are likely more excited and engaged by being proactively part of the solutions compared to coming on board at a later stage or compliance with (upcoming) legal requirements.

Patagonia, Interface, and TDC Net play leading roles in tackling climate change, gaining a significant competitive edge. Dycle in Berlin is an 'Innovator' in tackling the plastics crisis. We can expect to see a shift to 'Early adopters' and 'Early majority' in the coming years in this space, with 175 nations having agreed to develop a legally binding agreement on plastic pollution by 2024 following the UN resolution passed in 2022. Tony's Chocolonely leads on tackling child labour in the cocoa sector. Brigade and Beyond Food, Ctalents, Goodwill Solutions, and Grassroutes are innovators in empowering people out of poverty and social exclusion.

Sustainability adoption curve©

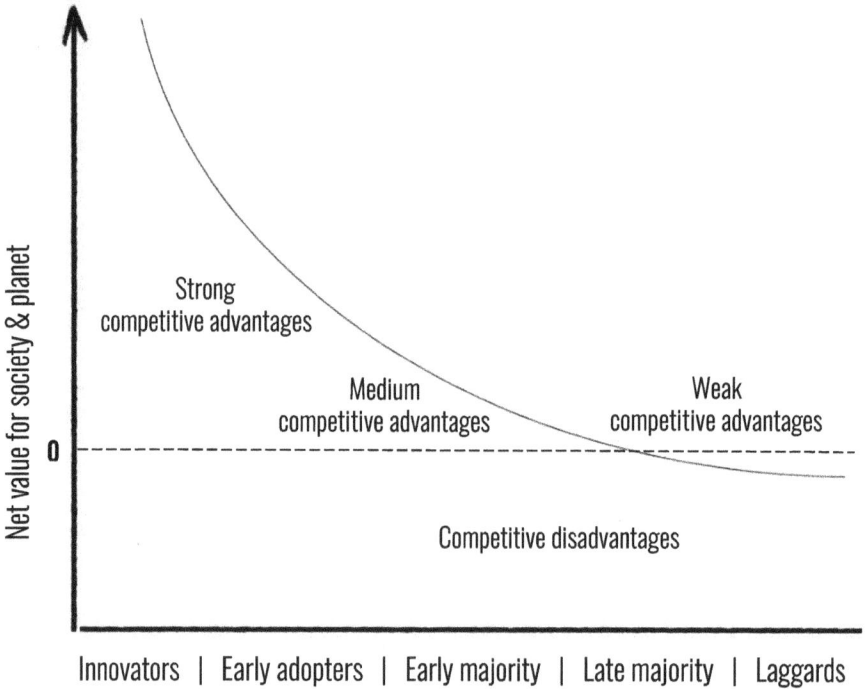

Net value for society & planet

Strong
competitive advantages

Medium
competitive advantages

Weak
competitive advantages

0 -

Competitive disadvantages

Innovators | Early adopters | Early majority | Late majority | Laggards

On a scale of 'depleting' versus 'maximising positive value' for society and planet where is your company positioned and where does it want to be?

Do you want your organisation to be part of the innovators, early adopters, early majority, late majority, or laggards in terms of tackling climate change, pollution, fixing poverty, social exclusion, or rising inequality?

IMPACT Wheel

Now that you have clarified your *'why'*, the vision you want to achieve, you can brainstorm *'how'* to achieve this vision.

The guiding questions and examples for each quadrant of the IMPACT Wheel outlined in Chapters Two to Five can be used to tease out potential impact initiatives that tackle the root cause of global and local issues. Those that help to 'close the tap' of the key challenges we face instead of dealing with the symptoms.

Once you have brainstormed impact initiatives using the IMPACT Wheel, you can prioritise the ideas. To develop and assess the ideas initially, you could consider asking questions such as:

1.   What does success look like in a 'beyond wildest dreams scenario'?

2.   What does success look like on a small scale?

3.   Does it have quick win potential? Does it have high impact potential?

4.   How well does the initiative align with your impact vision?

5.   Does it fit well with your business model?

6.   What are the costs involved in implementing the initiatives?

7.   What are the likely business benefits from implementing the improvements? (E.g., staff engagement loyalty, customer loyalty, referrals, attraction to investors.)

It is good to double-check initiatives against facts and reflect on where you can make the most significant impact. In prioritising initiatives, keeping the 80-20 rule in mind can be helpful. This 'Pareto principle' suggests that roughly 80% of the outcomes are generated by 20% of the causes in many scenarios. If reducing carbon emissions is an essential part of your strategy, you may want to focus on the 'hotspots' in your company or supply chain by focusing on the most significant contributors first.

It can be helpful to opt for a mix of quick wins to get some immediate results to gain momentum and medium / long-term initiatives that lead to more structural impact.

You want to define manageable steps to lead the business towards your vision. An effective roadmap considers priorities that are powerful and effective but that are also manageable.

As the Chinese proverb that Ray Anderson emphasised in one of his initial videos communicating their sustainability strategy throughout Interface: "A journey of a thousand miles begins with one step."

Impact roadmap

Skyscanner is one of the rare startups in Scotland's to have achieved unicorn status. Mark Logan, who drove its impressive growth as COO of Skyscanner, sees the adoption of the 'Lean Startup' method as one of the factors behind its success.

Mark uses the term 'fail fast' to describe this method. He explains how people can get attached to their idea and find it hard to be open to the thought that it might not work and can spend much time, energy, and investment in pursuing a new idea before realising it is not working in its current form. To have a better chance of success, it helps to adopt the 'fail fast' lens by believing that a strategy might not work and discovering this as quickly as possible and with minimum resources.

The same applies to new impact initiatives. To test and develop new ideas, it is best to focus on learning as 'lean' as possible to what extent the intended impact outcomes and commercial results are met. To do so, it is helpful to ask: 'How can we test the intended outcomes of the idea with minimum resources as fast as possible?'

As with any roadmap or programme management plan, it requires allocating clear ownership, responsibilities, and timelines. Particularly if a company aims to manage the implementation in house without consultants driving progress, it is critical to ensure that responsibilities are clearly allocated, progress is monitored systematically, and – crucially – that those responsible are given the time to drive and implement changes.

An effective impact roadmap includes answers to the following questions:

1.   What does impact success look like in the short and long term?

2.   What does commercial success look like in the short and long term?

3.   How can we test the impact and commercial goals with minimum resources as fast as possible?

4.   What are the key milestones?

5.   What are the key roles and responsibilities to make it a success, and who fulfils these roles?

6.   What are the main resources required to make the project successful? How will you fund these resources?

7.   How will you manage key stakeholder interests?

8.   What are the main barriers and risks, and how will you manage these? Remember the importance of 'whole systems thinking': can the initiative cause harm elsewhere? How will you prevent, mitigate, and or monitor this?

9.   What does progress management and reporting look like?

Business case

Becoming a more impactful, sustainable, purpose-driven organisation can bring significant business benefits.[187]

We saw Costco and Unilever creating between 300% and 400% more in terms of turnover growth and investor returns over seven years, compared to competitors with less positive impact. Tony's Chocolonely has taken on a market share in the cocoa sector at a fast rate, driven by high customer loyalty and referral rates. As a Deloitte study shows, purpose driven companies grow three times faster than their peers.[188]

GE claims that its brand value increased by $6 billion USD after launching its GE Eco imagination range. By creating a more positive impact, companies tend to see their productivity going up and are better able to attract more talented staff. In fact, 86% of millennials are even willing to consider a pay cut to work at a company with aligned values.[189]

---

[187] BlackRock, 2019; Deloitte, 2019; Morgan Stanley, 2018; Sisodia, Wolfe, and Sheth, 2014; Whelan, T., Kronthal-Sacco, R., 2019
[188] Deloitte, 2019;
[189] Workplace Culture Trends, 2018

"

Our costs are down, not up. Our products are better than ever. And the goodwill in the marketplace is astonishing. It is a better way to make a bigger profit. And a more legitimate one at that. One that is not coming at the expense of future generations and the expense of the Earth.

Ray Anderson, former Founder and CEO, Interface

In prioritising and communicating impact initiatives, clarifying a high-level business case is helpful. This can include direct and indirect impact aims, direct and indirect commercial benefits, costs, potential risks, and mitigation.

An initiative that aims to provide training or employment opportunities to refugees would directly impact the people who have fled their countries and their families, by improving their livelihoods, social integration, health and wellbeing. An indirect impact could be better acceptance and understanding of refugees in society and welfare savings.

Direct benefits of employing refugees include adding talented, productive, and motivated staff to your team. Studies indicate that people from a refugee background show lower sick leave rates and turnover rates.[190] Lower turnover is estimated to save 20% of an annual salary, depending on the type of job. Indirect benefits may include higher engagement and productivity of the rest of the team, improved customer loyalty and referral rates, as well as a competitive edge through deeper insights into refugees as a customer segment.

The costs could include language courses, translators, and other types of support, such as mentoring by other team members. To cover these costs, funds may be available in the form of government grants.

Risks may relate to not sufficiently understanding the support needs of people who have fled their country for them to be able to flourish and contribute their potential. To mitigate this, you could consider working with expert organisations with experience of empowering refugees.

---

[190] Fiscal Policy Institute, 2018

In developing your business case, you could consider the following categories as potential commercial benefits:

1.   Business growth, e.g., customer loyalty and referral rates, market share, ability to attract capital, PR, and goodwill.

2.   Productivity, e.g., lower absenteeism and turnover, ability to attract talented staff, wellbeing, engagement, and sales rates.

3.   Reduced risks, e.g., preventing stranded assets, anticipating new legislation, anticipating scarcity, and higher costs of raw materials.

4.   Cost savings, e.g., lower energy consumption, transport, material, and packaging costs.

5.   Innovation.

6.   Brand Value.

For a more elaborate business case, you could compare an initiative's costs, impact, benefits, and risks against 'doing nothing' or alternative options.

Impact metrics that matter

"Not everything that counts can be counted, and not everything that can be counted counts."
Attributed to Albert Einstein[191]

Like a ship navigating its way to a destination, it is helpful to monitor if you are still on course to decide whether to adjust your plans. Some metrics are more valuable than others. There are two types of reasons why an indicator can be valuable. First, 'learning metrics' can help us understand to what extent we achieve the intended outcomes and how we can improve things. Second, 'communication metrics' enable us to communicate progress – for example, to maintain momentum and buy-in.

In many cases, people tend to focus on communication metrics primarily because they tend to show where there is positive progress. Mark Logan, Chief Entrepreneurial Advisor to the Scottish Government and Skyscanner's former COO refers to these as 'vanity metrics'. He explains that when we are attached to a project, we can be drawn to communicating what is going well instead of learning where things are going less well, which could inform us where critical adjustments are needed. Or, in some cases, the need to end an initiative that is not working as intended.

Let's take the micro-credit loans by the Grameen Bank in Bangladesh as an example. A 'communication metric' would be the number of mothers and their families lifted across the poverty line. Grameen defines this metric as 'having three meals a day', 'sleeping on a mattress instead of on the ground' and 'children attending school' to indicate the poverty line.

---

[191] McKee, 2004, p.153

Based on these indicators, the bank has lifted more than 9 million mothers and their families out of poverty.[192] This represents a hugely inspirational communication metric that can help to gain further buy-in and support.

On the flip side, in order to evaluate and improve the initiative, it can help to develop other indicators aimed at learning what is working well and less well. For example, what are the success rates of the micro-businesses? How do different micro-businesses perform and endure? How well are the micro-businesses aligned with people's skills and talents? Metrics related to these questions would provide better insights into how the initiative could improve.

Some micro-businesses supported by Grameen, such as those renting mobile phones, have proven to be less resilient when larger players enter a local market. Data can help to innovate the model, by encouraging more resilient micro-businesses for example, or by supporting initiatives that can be run in partnership with other businesses or at a larger scale beyond micro-businesses by a team of mothers.

In defining the metrics, it is helpful to identify 'what' to measure and 'why' to see if you have a good balance between 'communication metrics' and 'learning metrics'.

In addition to hard figures, it can be invaluable to gain a deeper understanding by talking to key players involved and collecting stories. As Mark Kauw, Impact Officer at Moyee Coffee, says: "Understand your chain, your suppliers! In our case, that does not only mean investigating the figures from our desk, but wellies in the mud, talking to the farmers during the harvest, and gathering information through local fieldwork."[193]

---

[192] Yunus, 2007; Yunus, Moingeon, & Lehmann-Ortega, 2010
[193] The Impact Path, 2023

In terms of 'what' to measure, the following questions can be helpful in terms of measuring the 'before', 'during' and 'after' of an initiative or strategy:

1. To what extent are you creating a positive impact?

2. To what extent are you causing potential harm elsewhere?

3. To what extent are you achieving the intended business benefits?

4. To what extent are you impacting your commercial proposition?

5. How can you gain a deeper understanding and collect stories?

Aside from 'what' to measure and 'why', useful questions to consider are 'how' to gather relevant data and report the metrics, for example by using dashboards, indices, or reports; and 'how' and 'when' to communicate and review this information. Metrics only have merit if they are used for valuable communication purposes, or to guide decision makers to maintain, improve, pivot, or halt certain initiatives or practices.

To manage impact on people and planet effectively, it is essential to align and integrate impact metrics with the overall governance of a business.

At Grameen Bank staff targets do not only include traditional metrics such as repayment rates, but also include metrics related to the borrowers and their families crossing the poverty line. Another example is food company Danone, where 20% of the executive annual compensation is based on environmental and social targets.

Communicating impact

"There is no amount of slick advertising at any cost that we could have done that would have created the same goodwill in the marketplace. You talk about authenticity at its very, very best."

Ray Anderson, Founder Interface

Creating a positive impact can play a big part in boosting customer loyalty and referral figures, and in turn business growth.

When customers perceive your impact to be authentic, loyalty and referrals tend to improve organically. You can stimulate customer referrals further through 'refer a friend' type campaigns, such as Tony's Chocolonely giving customers a code to 'refer your buddy' for 15% off the purchase of a chocolate bar.

To encourage customer loyalty, models such as subscription, leasing, refilling, or return schemes can also work well. Examples are the 'Light as a Service' or the 'Cooling as a Service' model, the Coca-Cola reusable bottle return scheme, or the Algramo dispenser units to refill bottles with household products such as detergents.

Business leaders must decide how to position their impact versus their products or services to optimise the benefits to be gained. Superior customer loyalty and referral figures only materialise when customers value a product or service, regardless of its impact.

On a sunny day in Amsterdam, Willemijn Verloop, Founder of investment fund Rubio Impact Ventures, shares her insights based on her experience with entrepreneurs that aim to make a positive impact: "Trying to market a product on the impact value is quite risky. Many young entrepreneurs feel that if they can show their product is doing good for society, the consumers will come, and they forget they will first rate you on quality and price."

Willemijn continues: "Although the storytelling about your product is essential and the impact, trying to market the product purely on that, in my experience, will not help you grow. The marketing of your impact should be the 'cherry on the cake'."

In the B2B context (businesses selling to other businesses) in particular, positioning impact may work better as a 'small cherry on the cake'.

Steve Morgan, Director of Operations at Goodwill Solutions, stresses: "We feel we need to impress our customers with our commercial side first, impress them with our ability to meet their requirements from a service point of view, and then add our social impact as icing on the cake. Because their first focus is on their business and satisfying their customers. They need to be very careful before they engage us because if we don't do the job properly, there could be damage to their brand as well."

In developing an impact communications plan, it is helpful to consider the importance of your impact to each stakeholder. Often, customers visiting the Brigade Bar and Bistro near London Bridge in London do not realise the transformative impact of the restaurant on people's lives. It enables customers to, first and foremost, perceive the value in terms of the excellent food and ambiance. On the back of the menu, Brigade tells customers a bit more about its impact.

Temi, one of the customers in the restaurant, shares with me how she likes the subtle approach. She explains: "I think the way that Brigade writes it on their menu, 'this is what we do, but here is our social mission,' is a great way to interact with it naturally, and not too forceful."

While labels can help build trust amongst customers that the impact is genuine and authentic, there can also be suspicion of labels due to 'greenwashing' and 'fairwashing'. A global review by the Competition and Markets Authority of randomly selected websites found that 40% of online green claims could be misleading consumers. To tackle this issue, the European Green Deal states: "Companies making 'green claims' should substantiate these against a standard methodology to assess their environmental impact." Several countries have adopted codes that include criteria for truthful, substantiated, specific, unambiguous, accurate claims that consider the entire lifecycle of a product or service.

A good example of a label that is specific is carbon labelling. Logitech was the first consumer electronics company to commit to labelling all of its products with their carbon footprint measured in kilograms of carbon dioxide emissions (kg CO_2e) over a typical two-year period of usage. The footprint considers how raw materials are sourced, as well as manufacturing, packaging, shipping and distribution, energy usage by consumers, and end of life management of the product.

If all companies were to use carbon labels, buyers would have more clarity to compare products and make informed decisions.

As Bracken Darrell, former CEO of Logitech, says in his interview with Mark Fallows on the *Impossible Network* podcast: "Carbon labelling is important for consistent standards, we need to get it legislated for all products."[194]

Labels could be extended to include other harmful emissions such as dioxin and other toxic chemicals. Aside from the impact on our planet, labels could take the other three quadrants of the IMPACT Wheel into consideration, as to what extent a product positively or negatively impacts poverty, inequality, social exclusion, and health and wellbeing.

---

[194] Interview Bracken Darrell by Mark Fallows, The Impossible Network Podcast, https://theimpossiblenetwork.com/podcast/bracken-darrell/

Logitech's carbon transparency labelling.

Storytelling can be one of the most powerful ways to communicate impact. There are excellent examples of communicating impact in creative and effective ways. The uneven chunks of Tony's Chocolonely chocolate bars – as opposed to the traditional squares – spark curiosity and symbolise the inequality in our world.

Henk-Jan Beltman, former Chief Chocolate Officer at Tony's Chocolonely explains: "We wanted to make a chocolate bar that has a story intrinsic inside. So, the bar is unequally shared, like the world is unequally shared. And you get letters from moms that say, 'Just before the soccer training, I gave two pieces of chocolate to the kids, and I had to explain the fact that the world is unequally shared because your bars are unequally shared'. And that's great."

Tony's Chocolonely's uneven bar chunks symbolise our world's inequality.

Photography by davidboni.com.

In a nutshell

1. A vision is the ultimate end game. It is the compass for your journey. Defining an ambitious impact vision unleashes creativity and energy throughout an organisation.

2. *'A journey of a thousand miles begins with one step'*. To choose your next steps wisely for the best outcomes, you can use the guiding questions in the IMPACT Wheel and the examples in this book to tease out initiatives that tackle the root cause of our key global issues. Those that 'close the tap' and that create positive knock-on effects.

3. In line with the 'lean start-up' method, it is more likely to succeed by testing the outcomes of ideas at the smallest possible scale, costs, and timeframe. Developing the IMPACT roadmap will give you an effective plan with clear objectives, responsibilities, and timeframes.

4. Sketching a business case is a powerful tool to prioritise and communicate initiatives. It can include direct and indirect benefits (such as improved growth, productivity, brand value, and resilience), costs, potential risks, and mitigation.

5. To navigate the journey towards your impact vision, it helps to check if you are on course at regular intervals. To develop IMPACT metrics that matter, it is helpful to reflect on 'what' to measure, 'why', 'how', and 'when'. Dividing metrics into 'communication metrics' and 'learning metrics' is a good way to ensure that measurements are not only useful to communicate progress, but also to evolve and improve your initiatives.

6. To most customers, impact is the 'cherry on the cake' in their purchase motivation, with the product or service's value more critical. Impact can be positioned as 'a large or small cherry' to help increase customer loyalty and referral rates. Communicating impact effectively and authentically can be a powerful way to boost these loyalty and referral rates, and in turn business growth.

Final thoughts
What sets genius leaders apart?

"

It is pioneering a new way of doing business that serves a higher purpose.

Ray Anderson, Founder Interface, US

"

It is an advanced way of doing business.

Sandra Ballij, Founder and CEO of Ctalents, The Netherlands

"

Business success is just a case of numbers. It's a case of making sure you spend less than you bring in. That's all it is. But changing people's lives is something you can always remember.

Mike Britton, Founder Goodwill Solutions, UK

Ultimately, LEADING LIKE A GENIUS comes down to a new way of doing business. Those that create the best outcomes in terms of profits, as well as value for society, integrate a sound commercial model with core justice principles. Like the most famous geniuses in our history, they pursue two opposites as part of a whole. Providing positive value to society is not separate from their business or seen as 'giving back'. Instead, 'profits and purpose' are both an integral part of their business, with their purpose resting on core pillars of justice first and foremost. The nature of justice provides a clear compass for when to make decisions in favor of profits, or impact on society, even when it does not lead to a positive business case.

Yes, the overall business case for sustainability is increasingly strong. Particularly when measured longer-term, companies that create more positive value for planet and societies show better business growth, productivity, brand value, and resilience.[195] But that does not mean that each impact initiative has a positive business case. It is crucial to realise that a negative business case does not mean that an initiative is not justifiable. While charity is desirable, justice is enforceable. It can be justified even without a business case.

Patagonia chooses to absorb the additional cost of organic cotton to avoid the harm caused by traditional cotton production. Interface chose to achieve Net Zero by 2020 back in 1994, when it was not yet as important in attracting customer and talented staff, because 'it was the right thing to do'. TDC NET in Denmark chooses to be ahead of the Climate Paris Agreement as a leading example in the mobile communications sector. Costco applies a lower pay gap than its competitors. Tony's Chocolonely pays between 22% and 61% over the farm gate price. SoleRebels pays its workers more than three times the industry average. HISBE supermarket pays its suppliers 67% of the retail prices charged to customers.

Each of these decisions is tenable by the nature of justice.

---

[195] BlackRock, 2019; Deloitte, 2019; Kantar, 2020, Morgan Stanley, 2018; Sisodia, Wolfe, and Sheth, 2014; Whelan, T., Kronthal-Sacco, R., 2019

Most people hold freedom very dear. Freedom allows us to flourish and evolve. A society or market economy based on justice without freedom would restrict and stifle us and be inefficient. But a market economy based on freedom without justice destroys societies. To reiterate the words of Adam Smith: "Justice is the main pillar that upholds the whole edifice [free market economies]. If it is removed, the immense fabric of human society must crumble into atoms."[196]

Choosing to LEAD LIKE A GENIUS will ultimately make the difference between a future with more fires, floods, draughts, storms, and a further loss of biodiversity, or a future where we limit the impact of climate change. It will be the difference between the plastics crisis getting worse, or improving the quality of water in our rivers, seas, and oceans. It will be the difference between breathing polluted or cleaner air. It can change the reality of half of the people in our world who live in poverty struggling to meet basic needs, affecting children the most. And it will be the difference between an increasingly unequal world with consequences for all our mental and physical health, social unrest, more dysfunctional societies, and further polarization, a perfect breeding ground for populism. Or a future of living in more harmonious societies.

I believe that we can change things around and create a far better future than where we are currently heading. But what we need for things to genuinely turn around is for the right solutions, those that really work, to be more adopted by the mainstream.

Those who lead the way will ultimately reap the most significant competitive advantages. While perhaps not the easiest road to take, I have witnessed a sparkle in the eyes of all those who take it; and I have seen how it creates tremendous pride, and joy in their lives and of those around them. It is something that does not happen overnight and takes effort and commitment. But choosing to lead the way is vital for all of us, our children, and grandchildren to be able to live in a thriving and harmonious world.

---

[196] Smith, 1759: 84

"

Never doubt that a small group of thoughtful, committed citizens can change the world. Indeed, it's the only thing that ever has.

Margaret Mead

Contact

I hope that the examples and insights in this book have been helpful to you. As I keep learning please let me know if you have suggestions to improve (a future edition of) this book. You can reach me at hi@bigtreeglobal.net, or via LinkedIn.

If you would like to sign up to receive our updates and invitations to our webinars, or to find out more about our immersive impact trips, workshops, training, or coaching, please feel free to have a look at out our website www.bigtreeglobal.net.

If you enjoyed reading the book and would like to support it, I would be very grateful if you are happy to leave a review on the platform where you bought the book or share it with people who you think may like to read it.

Finally, I wish you much courage and joy on your path to make it as (positively) impactful as possible!

Melanie

References

AHDB. 2020. *UK farm gate milk prices*, https://ahdb.org.uk/dairy/uk-farmgate-milk-prices.

AHDB, 2023. *UK farm gate milk prices*, https://ahdb.org.uk/dairy/uk-farmgate-milk-prices.

Alvaredo, F., Chancel, L., Piketty, T., Saez, E., and Zuckman, G. 2018. *World Inequality Report*, Paris: World Inequality Lab.

Baron, J. 1996. Do no harm. In Messick, D., Tenbrunsel, A. (Eds.), *Codes of conduct: Behavioral research into business ethics*: 197-213. New York: Russell Sage Foundation.

Barton, D., Wiseman, M. 2014. Focusing capital on the long term. *Harvard Business Review,* 92: 44-51.

Barton, D., Wiseman, M. 2015. Perspectives on the Long Term, *McKinsey Quarterly*, March 2015.

BlackRock. 2018. Global Insights: Sustainable investing: A 'why not' moment. *Environmental, social and governance investing insights*, BlackRock Investment Institute, https://www.blackrock.com/corporate/literature/whitepaper/bii-sustainable-investing-may-2018-international.pdf.

BlackRock. 2019. Global Insurance Report. 2019. *Portfolio resilience through sustainability*, 23 Sep 2019, BlackRock Investment Institute, https://www.blackrock.com/institutions/en-gb/insights/investment-actions/global-insurance-report-2019/portfolio-resilience-through-sustainability.

BofAML. 2019. *ESG Matters: 10 reasons you should care about ESG*, 23 September 2019, Bank of America Merrill Lynch, https://www.bofaml.com/content/dam/boamlimages/documents/articles/ID19_1119/esg_matters.pdf.

Bosse, D., Harrison, J. 2011. Stakeholders, entrepreneurial rent and bounded self-interest. *Stakeholder Theory: Impact and Prospects, Cheltenham, UK: Edward Elgar*: 193-211.

Bramley, G., Hirsch, D., Littlewood, M., Watkins, D. 2016. *Counting the cost of UK poverty*, York: Joseph Rowntree Foundation.

Brandsen, T., Karré, P. 2011. Hybrid organizations: no cause for concern? *International Journal of Public Administration*, 34(13): 827-836.

Brewer, R. G., 2023. *Costco Reports a Majorly Successful Member Renewal Rate. Time to Buy?* The Motley Fool, Feb 2 2023, https://www.fool.com/investing/2023/02/02/costco-reports-a-majorly-successful-member-renewal/#:~:text=It%20wants%20members%20who%20sign,appear%20happy%20to%20remain%20customers.

Bruntland Commission. 1987. *Our Common Future*.

Chancel, L., Piketty, T., Saez, E., Zucman, G. et al. *World Inequality Report 2022,* World Inequality Lab, https://wir2022.wid.world/www-site/uploads/2022/01/Summary_WorldInequalityReport2022_English.pdf.

Chang, H. 2010. *23 Things they don't tell you about capitalism*. London: Penguin Books Ltd.

Cheeseman, G. 2012. *The Problem with the TOMS Shoes Charity Model*; https://www.triplepundit.com/story/2012/problem-toms-shoes-charity-model/66636.

Cho, S., Fang, X., Tayur, S., Xu, Y. 2017. *Combating Child Labour: Incentives and Information Disclosure in Global Supply Chains.* https://ssrn.com/abstract=2552268. Accessed 12 February 2018.

Climate Watch. 2023. https://www.climatewatchdata.org/, accessed 12 July 2023.

Coca-Cola. 2016. *The Coca-Cola Company: 2016 Sustainability Report,* https://www.coca-colacompany.com/content/dam/journey/us/en/policies/pdf/sustainability/2016-sustainability-report-the-coca-cola-company.pdf.

Collins, C., Porras, J. 1996. Leadership & Managing People, Building Your Company's Vision, From the September 1996 Issue, *Harvard Business Review.*

Comparably. 2023. https://www.comparably.com/competitors/costco-vs-walmart, accessed 22 July 2023.

Corbett, S., Fikkert, B. 2009. When Helping Hurts: Alleviating Poverty Without Hurting the Poor and Yourself, Moody Publishers, Chicago.

Cosic. 2017. *'We are all entrepreneurs': Muhammad Yunus on changing the world, one microloan at a time*. The Guardian. https://www.theguardian.com/sustainable-business/2017/mar/29/we-are-all-entrepreneurs-muhammad-yunus-on-changing-the-world-one-microloan-at-a-time.

Costco. 2022. Costco WholeSale 2022 Annual Report. https://s201.q4cdn.com/287523651/files/doc_financials/2022/ar/Costco-2022-Annual-Report.pdf

Crocker, J., Canevello, A. and Brown, A. 2017. Social motivation: Costs and benefits of selfishness and otherishness. *Annual review of psychology, 68*: 299-325.

Cunningham, S., Hudson, C.C. & Harkness, K., 2021, Social Media and Depression Symptoms: a Meta-Analysis. *Research on Child and Adolescent Psychopathology* 49, 241–253.

Currie, J. 2011. Inequality at Birth: Some Causes and Consequences', *American Economic Review*: Papers and Proceedings 101, 3: 1-22.

Davenport, C. 2012. *The Broken "Buy-One, Give-One" Model: 3 Ways To Save Toms Shoes.* https://www.fastcompany.com/1679628/the-broken-buy-one-give-one-model-three-ways-to-save-toms-shoes.

Deloitte. 2017. *The Deloitte millennial survey 2017: Apprehensive millennials: seeking stability and opportunities in an uncertain world,* https://www2.deloitte.com/global/en/pages/about-deloitte/articles/millennialsurvey.html.

Deloitte. 2019. *The price tag of plastic pollution.*
https://www2.deloitte.com/content/dam/Deloitte/my/Documents/risk/my-risk-sdg14-the-price-tag-of-plastic-pollution.pdf

Department for Work and Pensions. 2020. Households Below Average Income, Statistics on the number and percentage of people living in low income households for financial years 1994/95 to 2018/19, Table 4.3db.

Doucet, M., Guillemot, J., Lassonde, M., Gagné, J., Leclerc, C., Lepore, F. 2005. Blind subjects process auditory spectral cues more efficiently than sighted individuals. *Experimental brain research*, 160(2): 194-202.

Doward, J. 2020. *Children as young as eight picked coffee beans on farms supplying Starbucks*, The Guardian, 1 March 2020, https://www.theguardian.com/business/2020/mar/01/children-work-for-pittance-to-pick-coffee-beans-used-by-starbucks-and-nespresso.

Economic Times, The. 2020. *India added 3 billionaires a month in 2019; Mukesh Ambani richest Indian,* Feb 26, 2020, https://economictimes.indiatimes.com/markets/stocks/news/india-added-3-dollar-billionaires-a-month-in-2019-mukesh-ambani-richest-indian/articleshow/74323533.cms.

Edmonds, E., Schady, N. 2012. Poverty alleviation and child labour. *American Economic Journal: Economic Policy,* 4: 100-124.

EFRAC. 2016. House of Commons, Environment, Food and Rural Affairs Committee, Farm gate prices Third Report of Session 2015–16.

Ellen MacArthur Foundation. 2014. *Towards the circular economy*, vol. 3, Cowes.

Ellen MacArthur Foundation. 2017. The New Plastics Economy: Rethinking the future of plastics & catalysing action.

Ellen MacArthur Foundation, 2021. Case Study: Cooling as a service: Kaer, https://www.ellenmacarthurfoundation.org/circular-examples/cooling-as-a-service-kaer.

Ellen MacArthur Foundation, 2021. Case Study: Swedish Return System, An industry wide shared packaging system, https://archive.ellenmacarthurfoundation.org/case-studies/an-industry-wide-shared-packaging-system#:~:text=Each%20year%2C%20in%20comparison%20to,Sweden's%20Food%20industry%20in%202019.

Ellen MacArthur Foundation, 2021. Case Study: Universal Bottle from the Coca-Cola Company, A reusable bottle design for multiple brands, https://archive.ellenmacarthurfoundation.org/case-studies/a-reusable-drinks-bottle-design-for-multiple-brands.

Ellen MacArthur Foundation. 2022. https://ellenmacarthurfoundation.org/topics/plastics/overview.

Enamorado, T., López-Calva, L., Rodríguez-Castelán, C., Winkler, H. 2014. *Income inequality and violent crime, evidence from Mexico's drug war.* The World Bank, Poverty Reduction and Economic Management Unit.

Eon, 2020. *Sustainable shift: Consumers demand greener products in wake of pandemic.* https://www.companynewshq.com/company-news/personal-finance-utilities-company-news/sustainable-shift-consumers-demand-greener-products-in-wake-of-pandemic/.

EPA. 2023. Dioxin Key Facts, https://www.epa.gov/dioxin/learn-about-dioxin, last updated 1 June 2023.

Equality Trust. 2017. *Cost of inequality.* https://www.equalitytrust.org.uk/cost-inequality.

Erdal, D. 2014. *Employee ownership and health: an initial study.* In: Novkovic, S., and Webb, T. (eds) Co-operatives in a post-growth era: creating co-operative economics, London, Zed Books.

European Commission. 2015. Closing the loop: an EU action plan for the circular economy, Brussels, European Commission.

European Parliament. 2016. *Planned obsolescence: exploring the issues*, Brussels, European Parliament briefing.

Financial Times. 2018. *The profitable company that cares about the planet*, 17 May 2018, Rigby, R., https://www.ft.com/content/1564e99a-5766-11e8-806a-808d194ffb75.

Fiscal Policy Institute, 2018. Refugees as Employees: Good Retention, Strong Recruitment, May 2018, https://fiscalpolicy.org/wp-content/uploads/2018/05/Refugees-as-employees.pdf.

Flammer, C. 2015. Does corporate social responsibility lead to superior financial performance? A regression discontinuity approach. *Management Science, 61:* 2549-2568.

Fleming, M. 2020. *Consumers don't want to choose between sustainability and convenience*, https://www.marketingweek.com/brands-sustainability-convenience/.

Forbes, 2017. *This Law Firm Has Helped Deploy Over $500 Million In Impact Investments Worldwide.* https://www.forbes.com/sites/julianmitchell/2017/10/27/this-law-firm-has-helped-deploy-over-500-million-in-impact-investments-globally/#bce53534fd6c

Forbes. 2018. *88% Of consumers want you to help them make a difference.* https://www.forbes.com/sites/solitairetownsend/2018/11/21/consumers-want-you-to-help-them-make-a-difference/#d28f10f69547.

Forbes. 2019. *Case Study: SAP Shows How Employee Well-being Boosts The Bottom Line*, https://www.forbes.com/sites/jimpurcell/2019/10/28/case-study-sap-shows-how-employee-wellbeing-boosts-the-bottom-line/?sh=47448d8732a4.

Forbes. 2020. *Costco Is A Better Bet Than Walmart.* https://www.forbes.com/sites/greatspeculations/2020/08/14/costco-is-a-better-bet-than-walmart/.

Frazer, G. 2008. Used-clothing donations and apparel production in Africa. *The Economic Journal, 118*(532): 1764-1784.

Geyer, R., Jambeck, J., Law, K. 2017. Production, use, and fate of all plastics ever made. *Science Advances.* 3. e1700782. 10.1126/sciadv.1700782.

Gilbert, J. 2018. *Every CFO Should Know This: 'The Future Of Banking' Ties Verified ESG Performance To Cheaper Capital*, Forbes, Feb 20, 2018, https://www.forbes.com/sites/jaycoengilbert/2018/02/20/every-cfo-should-know-this-the-future-of-banking-ties-verified-esg-performance-to-cheaper-capital/#52bedc667e4d.

Global E-waste Monitor. 2020. https://www.itu.int/en/ITU-D/Environment/Pages/Spotlight/Global-Ewaste-Monitor-2020.aspx.

Godley. 2019. *Godley on the Fringe.* https://janeygodley.com/edinburgh-fringe.

Grameen Bank. 2017. *Grameen Bank's profit rises, interest declines* http://www.grameen.com/grameen-banks-profit-rises-interest-declines/, The Financial Express Published: 15 Aug 2017.

Grameen Bank, 2020. *Annual Report,* https://grameenbank.org.bd/public/assets/archive/annual_report/Annual_Report_2020-1_41.pdf

Grooten, M., Almond, R. 2018. *Living Planet Report - 2018: Aiming Higher.* WWF, Gland, Switzerland.

Grover, V., 2022. The Dilemma of Social-Media and Polarization Around the Globe. *Journal of Global Information Technology Management* 25:4, pages 261-265.

Hall, H., Griffiths, D., McKenna, L. 2013. From Darwin to constructivism: the evolution of grounded theory. *Nurse Researcher,* 20(3).

Harris-White, B. 2006. Poverty and capitalism. *Economic and Political Weekly,* 41: 1241-1246.

Hayek, F. 1976. *The Mirage of Social Justice.* Vol. 2 of Law, Legislation, and Liberty.

Herrera, A. 2013. *Questioning the TOMS Shoes model for social enterprise,* https://boss.blogs.nytimes.com/2013/03/19/questioning-the-toms-shoes-model-for-social-enterprise/?_r=0.

Hollender, J. 2010. *Less bad does not equal good: Seventh generation CEO Jeffrey Hollender.* https://www.fastcompany.com/video/less-bad-does-not-equal-good-seventh-generation-ceo-jeffrey-hollender/6MHOg2gU.

Horne, S., *Milk cost of production heads for 40p/litre and higher*, Farmers Weekly, 17 March 2022, https://www.fwi.co.uk/business/markets-and-trends/dairy-markets/milk-cost-of-production-heads-for-40p-litre-and-higher.

ICA. 2014. *World Cooperative Monitor.* International Cooperative Alliance, Geneva, ICA.

IEA. 2020. *Data Centres and Data Transmission Networks.* https://www.iea.org/reports/data-centres-and-data-transmission-networks.

ILO. 2014. International Labour Organisation (2014) Global Wage Report. Geneva, ILO.

ILO. 2017. *Global Estimates of Child Labour: Results and Trends 2012-2016*, Geneva, ILO, https://www.ilo.org/wcmsp5/groups/public/---dgreports/---dcomm/documents/publication/wcms_575499.pdf.

IMF. 2014. *Redistribution, inequality and growth*. IMF Staff Discussion note, February 2014.

IMF. 2019. *A strategy to protect whales can limit greenhouse gases and global warming*. Finance & Development, 56 (4), https://www.imf.org/external/pubs/ft/fandd/2019/12/natures-solution-to-climate-change-chami.htm.

Impact Investing Institute, 2022. *Sizing the Impact Investing Market 2022*, https://thegiin.org/assets/2022-Market%20Sizing%20Report-Final.pdf

Institute for Health Metrics and Evaluation. 2017. *Data life expectancy: Global burden of disease study 2016*. Institute for Health Metrics and Evaluation, University of Washington, Seattle. http://www.healthdata.org/sites/default/files/files/policy_report/2019/GBD_2017_Booklet.pdf. Accessed October 7, 2017.

Interface, 2016. *Interview with Ray Anderson*, Interface YouTube channel, 12 April 2016, https://www.youtube.com/watch?v=7eUMdcgXxJo.

IPCC. 2014. Climate Change 2014: Synthesis Report. Contribution of Working Groups I, II and III to the Fifth Assessment Report of the Intergovernmental Panel on Climate Change. IPCC, Geneva.

IPCC. 2018. Summary for Policymakers. In: Global Warming of 1.5°C. An IPCC Special Report on the impacts of global warming of 1.5°C above pre-industrial levels and related global greenhouse gas emission pathways, in the context of strengthening the global response to the threat of climate change, sustainable development, and efforts to eradicate poverty. World Meteorological Organization, Geneva, Switzerland: 32.

Jack, L., 2021. *FRC Food Policy Discussion Paper: The secrets of supermarketing: A model balanced on a knife edge*, University of Portsmouth.

Jambeck, R., Geyer, R., Wilcox, C., Siegler, T., Perryman, M., Andrady, A., Narayan, R., Law, K. 2015. Plastic waste inputs from land into the ocean. *Science,* 347(6223): 768-771.

Jiang, Y., Ekono, M., Skinner, C. 2016. *Basic Facts About Low-Income Children*. National Center for Children in Poverty. http://www.nccp.org/publications/pub_1145.html.

John Lewis. 2011. *The John Lewis Partnership Bond*, www.partnershipbond.vom/content/jlbond/about.html.

Jung, H. & Lee, S., 2023. Social media use and polarized redistributive attitudes: a comparative and causal perspective. *Information, Communication & Society,* 0:0, pages 1-21.

Kantar. 2020. *Purpose 2020, Inspiring Purpose-led growth*, https://kantar.no/globalassets/ekspertiseomrader/merkevarebygging/purpose-2020/p2020-frokostseminar-250418.pdf.

Karmali, N. 2010. *Aravind Eye Care's Vision for India*. https://www.forbes.com/global/2010/0315/companies-india-madurai-blindness-nam-familys-vision.html#3d189c0d5c7e, Forbes, March 5, 2010.

Karnani, A. 2014. Corporate social responsibility does not avert the tragedy of the commons. Case study: Coca-Cola India. *Economics, Management and Financial Markets*, 9: 11.

Karns, C., Dow, M., Neville, H. 2012. Altered cross-modal processing in the primary auditory cortex of congenitally deaf adults: a visual-somatosensory fMRI study with a double-flash illusion. *Journal of Neuroscience*, 32(28): 9626-9638.

Kelly, M. 2000. Inequality and crime. *The Review of Economics and Statistics*, 82: 530-539.

Kelly, M. 2003. The divine right of capital: Dethroning the corporate aristocracy. San Franciso: Berrett-Koehler Publishers.

Kiedrowski, N., 2023. *2 Retail Stocks to Buy Today*, Stock News, Oct 13 2023, https://stocknews.com/news/cost-hd-2-retail-stocks-to-buy-today/

Klein, N., 2014. *This changes everything: capitalism vs. the climate*. Toronto, Canada: Random House.

Kubin, E. & von Sikorski, C., 2021. The role of (social) media in political polarization: a systematic review, *Annals of the International Communication Association*, 45:3, 188-206.

Legislation.go.uk, 2012. *Public Services (Social Value) Act 2012*, https://www.legislation.gov.uk/ukpga/2012/3/enacted.

Lomborg, B. 2015. *Copenhagen Consensus Center Nobel Laureates Guide to Smarter Global Targets to 2030.* https://www.copenhagenconsensus.com/post-2015-consensus/nobel-laureates-guide-smarter-global-targets-2030.

Luke, B., Barraket, J., Eversole, R. 2013. Measurement as legitimacy versus legitimacy of measures: Performance evaluation of social enterprise. *Qualitative Research in Accounting & Management*, 10: 234-258.

Lush.com, 2023. *Going Naked: A Money and Planet Saving Solution*, https://weare.lush.com/press-releases/going-naked-a-money-and-planet-saving-solution/.

Macey, J., 2014. Crony capitalism: Right here, right now. Harvard Journal of Law and Public Policy, 37(1), 5–9.

Maiese, M. 2020. 2003. *"Principles of Justice and Fairness."* Beyond Intractability. Eds. Guy Burgess and Heidi Burgess. Conflict Information Consortium, University of Colorado, Boulder. http://www.beyondintractability.org/essay/principles-of-justice.

Maitre-Ekern, E., Dalhammar, C. 2016. Regulating planned obsolescence: a review of legal approaches to increase product durability and reparability in Europe. *Review of European, Comparative & International Environmental Law*, 25(3): 378-394.

Malm, A., 2015. *Exploding in the air: beyond the carbon trail of neoliberal globalisation*. In: L. Pradella and T. Marois, eds. Polarizing development: alternatives to neoliberalism and the crisis. London: Pluto Press, 108-118.

Mandela, N. 2005. *Nelson Mandela, Make Poverty History Speech*. Trafalgar Square, London
https://www.youtube.com/watch?v=le0tRVRZCOQ.

Mandela, N. 2013. *Nelson Mandela, Speech on Poverty.*
https://www.youtube.com/watch?v=tevKVIcHscw.

Manjit, J. 2019. *Why corporates' ESG data matters to investors.* Insight, 20-11-2019,
https://www.robecosam.com/csa/insights/2019/why-corporates-esg-data-matters-to-
investors.html.

Marino, C., Gini, G., Vieno, A., & Spada, M. M., 2018. The associations between problematic
Facebook use, psychological distress and well-being among adolescents and young adults:
A systematic review and meta-analysis. *Journal of Affective Disorders*, 226, 274–281.
Elsevier B.V.

McAuley. 2016. 'France becomes the first country to ban plastic plates and cutlery',
Washington Post, 19 September.

McAuley, R. 2007. Out of sight: Crime, youth and exclusion in modern Britain, Willan.

McCarty, N., Poole, K., Rosenthal, H., 2003. Political polarization and income
inequality. *Available at SSRN 1154098.*

McCrae, N., Gettings, S., & Purssell, E., 2017. Social media and depressive symptoms in
childhood and adolescence: A systematic review. *Adolescent Research Review.*

McKee, M., 2004. Not everything that counts can be counted; not everything that can be
counted counts. *BMJ, 328*(7432): 153.

Méle, D. 2009. Integrating personalism into virtue-based business ethics: The personalist
and the common good principles. *Journal of Business Ethics*, 88(1): 227-244.

Miller, D. 2017. *Justice: The Stanford encyclopaedia of philosophy.*
https://plato.stanford.edu/archives/fall2017/entries/justice. Metaphysics Research Lab.
Stanford University.

Mintzberg, H., Simons, R., Basu, K. 2002. Beyond Selfishness. *MIT Sloan Management
Review*, 44(1): 67.

Monbiot, G., 2017. *Out of the wreckage: a new politics for an age of crisis.* London: Verso.

Moore, J.W., 2015. *Capitalism in the web of life: ecology and the accumulation of capital.*
New York: Verso.

Nelson, V., Phillips, D. 2018. Sector, landscape or rural transformations? Exploring the
limits and potential of agricultural sustainability initiatives through a cocoa case study.
Business Strategy and the Environment, 27: 252-262.

Nicholson, C., Young, B. 2012. The relationship between supermarkets and suppliers: What
are the implications for consumers? *Consumers International, Europe Economics*, July
2012.

Nilsson, M., Schenkman, B. 2016. Blind people are more sensitive than sighted people to
binaural sound-location cues, particularly inter-aural level differences. *Hearing research*,
332: 223-232.

Nkamleu, G., Kielland, A. 2006. Modeling farmers' decisions on child labour and schooling in the cocoa sector: a multinomial logit analysis in Côte d'Ivoire. *Agricultural Economics,* 35: 319-333.

Noble, M. 2017. Chocolate and the consumption of forests: A cross-national examination of ecologically unequal exchange in cocoa exports. *Journal of World-Systems Research,* 23: 236-268.

NORC, 2020. *NORC Final Report: Assessing Progress in Reducing Child Labor in Cocoa Production in Cocoa Growing Areas of Côte d'Ivoire and Ghana*, University of Chicago, October 2020, https://www.norc.org/content/dam/norc-org/documents/standard-projects-pdf/NORC%202020%20Cocoa%20Report_English.pdf.

Obama, B. 2013. *Remarks by the President on Economic Mobility*, The White House, Office of the Press Secretary, December 04, 2013, https://obamawhitehouse.archives.gov/the-press-office/2013/12/04/remarks-president-economic-mobility#:~:text=And%20that%20is%20a%20dangerous,works%20for%20every%20working%20American.

OECD. 2014. '*Trends in Income Inequality and its Impact on Economic Growth*'. OECD Social, Employment and Migration Working Papers, no. 163, Paris, OECD publishing.

OECD. 2015. *In It Together: Why Less Inequality Benefits All*. Paris: OECD Publishing. http://dx.doi.org/10.1787/9789264235120-en.

OECD. 2016. *Society at a glance 2016: OECD social indicators.* Paris, OECD Publishing. http://www.oecd-ilibrary.org.ezproxy.lib.gla.ac.uk/social-issues-migration-health/society-at-a-glance_19991290.

OECD/ IEA. 2016. *World Energy Outlook Special Report,* International Energy Agency, Paris, France, www.iea.org, http://pure.iiasa.ac.at/id/eprint/13467/1/WorldEnergyOutlookSpecialReport2016EnergyandAirPollution.pdf.

OECD. 2017. *World Inequality Database.* http://www.oecd.org/social/inequality.htm, accessed 30 June 2017.

OECD, 2018, *Improving Plastics Management: Trends, policy responses, and the role of international co-operation and trade,* https://www.oecd.org/environment/waste/policy-highlights-improving-plastics-management.pdf

OECD. 2020. *OECD Income Distribution Database (IDD): Gini, poverty, income, Methods and Concepts*, http://www.oecd.org/social/income-distribution-database.htm.

OECD.2022. *Global Plastics Outlook: Economic Drivers, Environmental Impacts and Policy Options,* https://www.oecd-ilibrary.org/environment/global-plastics-outlook_de747aef-en, accessed 12 July 2023.

OurWorldInData, 2017. *Oil Spills.* https://ourworldindata.org/oil-spills.

OurWorldInData. 2018. *The Ozone Layer.* https://ourworldindata.org/ozone-layer.

OurWorldInData. 2019. *CO$_2$ and other greenhouse gas emissions*, Oxford University, https://ourworldindata.org/co2-and-other-greenhouse-gas-emissions.

OurWorldInData. 2020a. *Global Extreme Poverty*, https://ourworldindata.org/extreme-poverty.

OurWorldInData. 2020b. *Deaths from COVID-19*, https://ourworldindata.org/coronavirus.

OurWorldInData. 2020c. *Sector by sector: where do global greenhouse gas emissions come from?* https://ourworldindata.org/ghg-emissions-by-sector.

OurWorldInData. 2020d. *The carbon footprint of foods: are differences explained by the impacts of methane?* https://ourworldindata.org/carbon-footprint-food-methane#licence.

OurWorldInData, 2023. https://ourworldindata.org/emissions-by-sector, accessed 12 July 2023.

Oxfam. 2020a. *Time to care: Unpaid and underpaid care work and the global inequality crisis*, Oxfam Briefing Paper January 2020, https://www.oxfamnovib.nl/Files/rapporten/2020/2020120%20bp-time-to-care-inequality-200120-embargo-en.pdf.

Oxfam. 2020b. *Confronting Carbon Inequality: Putting climate justice at the heart of the COVID-19 recovery.* 21 September 2020. https://oxfamilibrary.openrepository.com/bitstream/handle/10546/621052/mb-confronting-carbon-inequality-210920-en.pdf.

Oxford Dictionaries. 2017. www.oxforddictionaries.com.

Pachauri, R., Meyer, L. 2014. Fifth assessment report (AR5): Bali: Intergovernmental panel on climate change.

Padmanathan, P., Bould, H., Winstone, L., Moran, P., Gunnell, D., 2020. Social media use, economic recession and income inequality in relation to trends in youth suicide in high-income countries: a time trends analysis, *Journal of Affective Disorders*, Volume 275, 2020, 58-65.

Partridge, J. and Butler, S., 2023. *Dairy farmers quit in fury amid UK price squeeze and rising costs*, The Observer, 29 July 2023, https://www.theguardian.com/business/2023/jul/29/uk-dairy-farmers-costs-milk-price-energy-feed-bills.

Parvez, Sarker M., et al. 2021. *Health consequences of exposure to e-waste: an updated systematic review.* Lancet Planet Health, December 2021, 5: e905-20. https://www.thelancet.com/journals/lanplh/article/PIIS2542-5196(21)00263-1/fulltext.

Patagonia. 2011. *Patagonia advertisement from the Friday, November, 25, 2011 edition of The New York Times,* https://www.patagonia.com/stories/dont-buy-this-jacket-black-friday-and-the-new-york-times/story-18615.html.

Patagonia. 2020. https://eu.patagonia.com/gb/en/stories/dont-buy-this-jacket-black-friday-and-the-new-york-times/story-18615.html.

Philips. 2015. Philips provides Light as a Service to Schiphol Airport, Philips introduces light as a service at Schiphol supporting the transition to a circular economy. https://www.philips.com/a-w/about/news/archive/standard/news/press/2015/20150416-Philips-provides-Light-as-a-Service-to-Schiphol-Airport.html, April 16, 2015.

Philips, 2017. *Schiphol Airport opts for Circular lighting: a responsible choice*, Philips Lighting Holding B.V., https://www.assets.signify.com/is/content/PhilipsConsumer/PDFDownloads/Global/Case-studies/CSLI20170418_001-UPD-en_AA-Case-Study-LaaS-Schiphol.pdf.

Piketty, T. 2014. *Capital in the twenty-first century.* London: The Belknap Press of Harvard University Press.

Piketty, T., & Goldhammer, A. (2020). *Capital and ideology.* The Belknap Press of Harvard University Press.

Polman, P., & Winston, A. S. 2021. *Net positive: how courageous companies thrive by giving more than they take.* Boston, MA, Harvard Business Review Press.

Poole, M., Van de Ven, A. 1989. Using paradox to build management and organization theories. *Academy of Management Review*, 14(4): 562-578.

Porter, M., Kramer, R. 2011. Creating Shared Value. *Harvard Business Review,* 89: 62-77.

PwC. 2015a. *Make it your business: Engaging with the Sustainable Development Goals,* www.pwc.com/sdg, https://www.pwc.com/gx/en/sustainability/SDG/SDG%20Research_FINAL.pdf.

PwC. 2015b. *Making a difference: The social impact of Brigade.* https://www.pwc.co.uk/assets/pdf/brigade-sroi-report.pdf. Accessed 20 February, 2017.

PwC. 2020. *Total Impact,* https://www.pwc.com/totalimpact, accessed 12 June, 2020.

Ramdas, K. 2022. *Achieving The Inconceivable: Why Organizations That Challenge The Status Quo Succeed*, June 27 2022, https://www.forbes.com/sites/lbsbusinessstrategyreview/2022/06/27/achieving-the-inconceivable-why-organizations-that-challenge-the-status-quo-succeed/

Reichheld, A., Peto, J., Ritthaler, C. 2023. Consumers' Sustainability Demands Are Rising, *Harvard Business Review*, September 18, 2023.

Reinhardt, F., Casadesus-Masanell, R. and Kim, H. 2010. Patagonia. *Harvard Business School Strategy Unit Case*, (711-020).

Ries, E. 2011. The Lean Startup: How Today's Entrepreneurs Use Continuous Innovation to Create Radically Successful Businesses. New York, Crown Business.

Rogers, E. M. 1962. Diffusion of innovations. New York, Free Press of Glencoe.

Rosling, H., Rosling, O., Rosling Rönnlund, A. 2018. *Factfulness*, London, Hodder & Stoughton Ltd.

Rothschild, E., 2023, *Adam Smith, Climate and Loss*, Center for History and Economics, Harvard University, June 2023, https://histecon.fas.harvard.edu/climate-loss/smith/index.html

Russel Trust. 2016. *'Foodbank use remains at record high'*, 15 April 2016.

Russel Trust, 2023. End of Year Stats, https://www.trusselltrust.org/news-and-blog/latest-stats/end-year-stats/.

SAP. 2022. SAP Integrated Report 2022, https://www.sap.com/integrated-reports/2022/en.html.

Schad, J., Lewis, M., Raisch, S., Smith, W. 2016. Paradox research in management science: Looking back to move forward. *The Academy of Management Annals*, 10(1): 5-64.

Schiphol Group. 2022. Sustaining Your World: Vision and strategy towards the most sustainable airports. https://www.schiphol.nl/en/schiphol-group/page/road-to-the-most-sustainable-airports/

Sciencebasedtargets.org. 2023. https://sciencebasedtargets.org, accessed 13 July 2023.

Sen, A. 1999. *Development as Freedom.* Oxford: Oxford University Press.

Shikwati, J. 2005. For God's Sake, Please Stop the Aid. *Spiegel Online.*

Sisodia, R., Wolfe, D., Sheth, J. 2014. F*irms of Endearment: How World-Class Companies Profit from Passion and Purpose*, Pearson Education, Upper Saddle River, New Jersey.

Sky News, 2021. *ABBA star Björn Ulvaeus: Waterloo took us from rat race - I wish that for other songwriters*, 5 May 2021, https://news.sky.com/story/abba-star-bjoern-ulvaeus-waterloo-took-us-from-rat-race-i-wish-that-for-other-songwriters-12297381.

Sladen, D., Tharpe, A., Ashmead, D., Grantham, D., Chun, M. 2005. Visual attention in deaf and normal hearing adults. *Journal of Speech, Language, and Hearing Research*. 48: 1529–1537.

Smart Prosperity Institute, 2021. *Circular Economy Global Best Practices Series*, https://institute.smartprosperity.ca/sites/default/files/Automobile_Best%20Practices.pdf.

Smith, A. 1759. 2010. *The Theory of Moral Sentiments*. LA, CA, Enhanced Media Publishing.

Smith, A. 1776. 2012. *Wealth of Nations*. Hertfordshire, Wordsworth Editions Limited.

Smith, B. 2009. Awareness, interest, sensitivity, and advocacy-AISA: An educational 'take-away' for business ethics students. *American Journal of Business Education*, 2(9): 109-116.

Smith, W., Lewis, M. 2011. Toward a theory of paradox: A dynamic equilibrium model of organising. *Academy of Management Review*, 36(2): 381-403.

Smith, W., Tracey, P., 2016. Institutional complexity and paradox theory: Complementarities of competing demands. *Strategic Organization*, 14(4): 455-466.

Social Metrics Commission. 2019. *Measuring Poverty 2019, A report of the Social Metrics Commission*, July, 2019, https://socialmetricscommission.org.uk/wp-content/uploads/2019/07/SMC_measuring-poverty-201908_full-report.pdf.

Statista. 2020. *Distribution of average monthly income in households across India in 2015,* https://www.statista.com/statistics/653897/average-monthly-household-income-india/.

Stiglitz, J. 2013. *The Price of Inequality* London: Penguin Books Ltd.

Stuart, R. 2021. *Scooping Plastic Out of the Ocean Is a Losing Game,* Hakai Magazine Coastal science and societies, https://hakaimagazine.com/features/scooping-plastic-out-of-the-ocean-is-a-losing-game/

Swedo, E. A., Beauregard, J. L., de Fijter, S., Werhan, L., Norris, K., Montgomery, M. P., Rose, E. B., David-Ferdon, C., Massetti, G. ., Hillis, S. D., Sumner, S. A., Associations Between Social Media and Suicidal Behaviors During a Youth Suicide Cluster in Ohio, *Journal of Adolescent Health,*Volume 68, Issue 2, 2021, 308-316.

Swiers, K., 2023. Mark Vletter gives his company Voys away: 'I don't need those millions.' MT Sprout, 27 October 2023, https://mtsprout.nl/groei/mark-vletter-steward-ownership.

Taiichi, Ohno. 2006. *"Ask 'why' five times about every matter.",* archived from the original on Nov 27, 2022. Accessed 20 October, 2023.

TDC NET Case Study. 2023. Sciencebasedtargets.org, https://sciencebasedtargets.org/companies-taking-action/case-studies/net-zero-case-study-tdc-net, accessed 13 July 2023.

Tett, G., Nauman, B., Temple-West, P., Edgecliffe-Johnson, A. 2020. *ESG shines in the crash; legal milestone for ratings,* Financial Times, March 16 2020, https://www.ft.com/content/dd47aae8-ce25-43ea-8352-814ca44174e3.

Timmerman, K. 2023. *The problem with TOMS shoes & its critics.* Accessed 19 October, 2023. https://whereamiwearing.com/2011/04/toms-shoes/.

The Guardian. 2019. *We lose so many': the threefold tragedy of babies, mothers and abortion in Kibera.* https://www.theguardian.com/global-development/2019/aug/05/we-lose-so-many-women-the-tragedy-of-unsafe-abortion-in-kibera.

Thomas, S. 2012. '*The great recovery',* RSA blog.

The Impact Path, accessed 20 October 2023, https://www.eur.nl/en/ice/media/2020-06-impact-path.

ThredUp. 2020. *2020 Resale Report.* https://www.thredup.com/resale/#consumer-trends.

Tony's Chocolonely Annual Report. 2018. *Tony's Annual Year Report 2016/2017 'Jaarfairslag',* https://tonyschocolonely.com/storage/configurations/tonyschocolonelycom.app/files/jaarfairslag/2016-2017/tonys_annualfairreport_1617_en.pdf.

Tony's Chocolonely Annual Report. 2022. *Tony's Annual Year Report 2021/2022 'Jaarfairslag',* https://tonyschocolonely.com/uk/en/annual-fair-reports/annual-fair-report-2021-2022

Triodos. 2022. *Renumeration Engagement.* https://www.triodos-im.com/articles/2022/remuneration-engagement.

Twenge, J. M., Cooper, A. B., Joiner, T. E., Duffy, M. E., & Binau, S. G., 2019. Age, period, and cohort trends in mood disorder indicators and suicide-related outcomes in a nationally representative dataset, 2005–2017. *Journal of Abnormal Psychology*, 128(3), 185–199.

UNESCO. 2022. UNESCO Digital Library, accessed Nov 2022, https://unesdoc.unesco.org/ark:/48223/pf0000382577.

Unilever. 2018. *Unilever's Sustainable Living Plan continues to fuel growth,* https://www.unilever.com/news/press-releases/2018/unilevers-sustainable-living-plan-continues-to-fuel-growth.html.

United Nations. 2015. *Sustainable development goals knowledge platform,* https://sustainabledevelopment.un.org/sdgs.

United Nations. 2015a. https://news.un.org/en/story/2015/12/519172-sustainable-development-goals-kick-start-new-year, 30 Dec 2015.

United Nations. 2015b. *Transforming our world: The 2030 Agenda for Sustainable Development,* A/RES/70/1, United Nations, 2015, sustainabledevelopment.un.org.

United Nations. 2017a. *Leaded petrol phase-out: Global status as at March 2017.* https://www.unenvironment.org/explore-topics/transport/what-we-do/partnership-clean-fuels-and-vehicles/lead-campaign.

United Nations. 2017b. *Ozone data access center: ODS consumption in ADP tonnes.* https://unstats.un.org/unsd/environment/ODS_Consumption.htm.

United Nations. 2019. *The 2019 United Nations Global Compact Accenture Strategy CEO Study on Sustainability.* https://d306pr3pise04h.cloudfront.net/docs/publications/2019-UNGC-Accenture-CEO-Study.pdf.

United Nations. 2021. *UN Environmental Programme Report From Pollution to Solution: a global assessment of marine litter and plastic pollution*, October 2021.

United Nations Global Stocktake. 2023. *Synthesis Report UN Global Stocktake September 2023,* https://unfccc.int/topics/global-stocktake.

US Census Bureau, 2022. *Poverty Rate of Children Higher Than National Rate, Lower for Older Populations*, October 04, 2022, https://www.census.gov/library/stories/2022/10/poverty-rate-varies-by-age-groups.html#:~:text=The%20child%20poverty%20rate%20(for,lower%20than%20the%20national%20rate.

Verburg, R., 2018. *Greed, Self-Interest and the Shaping of Economics.* Routledge.

Vytal.org, 2023. Accessed 20October 2023, https://en.vytal.org/about/hygiene.

WEAll, 2023. *Mondragón Corporation – Employee Ownership*, accessed 20 October 2023, https://weall.org/resource/mondragon-corporation-employee-ownership.

Wharton, 2023. *In Ethiopia, Trading Poverty for Prosperity Provides Global Success for SoleRebels*, A business journal from the Wharton School of the University of Pennsylvania, accessed 19 October, 2023, https://knowledge.wharton.upenn.edu/article/in-ethiopia-trading-poverty-for-prosperity-provides-global-success-for-solerebels/.

Wilcox, L. 2020. *A MARKET-CREATION STORY: ARAVIND EYE CARE*, The Forum at Harvard Business School, https://www.hbs.edu/forum-for-growth-and-innovation/blog/Pages/default.aspx?post=51.

Wilkinson, R., Pickett, K. 2009. The Spirit Level: Why More Equal Societies Almost Always Do Better, London, Allen Lane.

Winkler, H. 2019. The effect of income inequality on political polarization: Evidence from European regions, 2002–2014. *Economics & Politics*, *31*(2): 137-162.

Winston, A. 2019. Is the Business Roundtable Statement Just Empty Rhetoric? *Harvard Business Review, Economics & Society*, 30 August 2019.

World Bank. 2017. *Poverty and shared prosperity*. http://www.worldbank.org/en/publication/poverty-and-shared-prosperity.

World Bank. 2018a. *Nearly Half the World Lives on Less than $5.50 a Day*, 17 October, 2018, https://www.worldbank.org/en/news/press-release/2018/10/17/nearly-half-the-world-lives-on-less-than-550-a-day?cid=EXT_WBEmailShare_EXT.

World Bank. 2018b. *Gini Index*, https://data.worldbank.org/indicator/SI.POV.GINI.

World Bank. 2020a. *Projected poverty impacts of COVID-19 (coronavirus)*. https://www.worldbank.org/en/topic/poverty/brief/projected-poverty-impacts-of-COVID-19.

World Bank. 2020b. *Poverty & Equity Brief, South Asia, India*, April 2020. https://databank.worldbank.org/data/download/poverty/987B9C90-CB9F-4D93-AE8C-750588BF00QA/SM2020/Global_POVEQ_IND.pdf.

World Economic Forum. 2020. *The Global Risks Report 2020*, Insight Report, 15th Edition, http://www3.weforum.org/docs/WEF_Global_Risk_Report_2020.pdf.

World Health Organization. 2016. *Dioxins and their effects on human health,* https://www.who.int/news-room/fact-sheets/detail/dioxins-and-their-effects-on-human-health, 4 October 2016.

World Health Organisation. 2018. *Climate change and health,* February 2018, https://www.who.int/news-room/fact-sheets/detail/climate-change-and-health.

World Health Organisation. 2022. *Children and E-Waste: Key Messages*, https://www.who.int/publications/i/item/WHO-HEP-ECH-CHE-22.04.

World Health Organisation, 2023a, Air Quality and Health, Health impacts, https://www.who.int/teams/environment-climate-change-and-health/air-quality-and-health/health-impacts, accessed 14 July 2023.

World Health Organisation, 2023b, Exposure & health impacts of air pollution, https://www.who.int/teams/environment-climate-change-and-health/air-quality-and-health/health-impacts/exposure-air-pollution.

World Inequality Database. 2020. https://wid.world.

World Resources Institute. 2023. https://www.wri.org/insights/4-charts-explain-greenhouse-gas-emissions-countries-and-sectors, accessed 12 July 2023.

WTTC. 2019. *Economic Impact Reports*. World Travel and Tourism Council & Oxford Economics.

Wright, C., Nyberg, D. 2017. An inconvenient truth: How organizations translate climate change into business as usual. *Academy of Management Journal*, 60(5): 1633–1661.

WWF. 2020. *WWF Living Planet Report 2020*, https://www.wwf.org.uk/sites/default/files/2020-09/LPR20_Full_report.pdf.

WWF. 2022 *Living Planet Report 2022 – Building a nature-positive society*. Almond, R.E.A., Grooten, M., Juffe Bignoli, D. & Petersen, T.

Wydick, B., Katz, E., Janet, B. 2014. 'Do In-Kind Transfers Damage Local Markets? The Case of TOMS Shoe Donations in El Salvador', University of San Francisco, March 12, 2014.

York, J., Hargrave, T., Pacheco, D. 2016. Converging winds: Logic hybridization in the Colorado wind energy field. *Academy of Management Journal*, 59(2): 579–610.

Yunus, M. 2007. Creating a world without poverty: Social business and the future of capitalism, New York: Public Affairs.

Yunus, M., Moingeon, B., Lehmann-Ortega, L. 2010. Building social business models: Lessons from the Grameen experience. *Long Range Planning,* 43: 308-325.

Zallio, M., Berry, D. 2017. Design and Planned Obsolescence: Theories and Approaches for Designing Enabling Technologies. *The Design Journal*, 20: sup1, S3749-S3761, DOI: 10.1080/14606925.2017.1352879.

Index